IN THE LOCKER ROOM

IN THE LOCKER ROOM

TALES OF THE PITTSBURGH STEELERS FROM THE
PLAYING FIELD TO THE BROADCAST BOOTH

TUNCH ILKIN WITH SCOTT BROWN

TRIUMPH
BOOKS

Library of Congress Cataloging-in-Publication Data

Names: Ilkin, Tunch, author. | Brown, Scott, author.
Title: In the locker room: tales of the Pittsburgh Steelers from the playing
    field to the broadcast booth / Tunch Ilkin, with Scott Brown.
Description: Chicago, Illinois : Triumph Books LLC, [2018]
Identifiers: LCCN 2018016982 | ISBN 9781629375021
Subjects: LCSH: Pittsburgh Steelers (Football team)—Anecdotes. | Pittsburgh
    Steelers (Football team)—History.
Classification: LCC GV956.P57 I53 2018 | DDC 796.332/640974886—dc23
LC record available at https://lccn.loc.gov/2018016982

This book is available in quantity at special discounts for your group or organization. For further information, contact:
Triumph Books LLC
814 North Franklin Street
Chicago, Illinois 60610
(312) 337-0747
www.triumphbooks.com

Printed in U.S.A.
ISBN: 978-1-62937-502-1
Design by Meghan Grammer
Page production by Nord Compo
Photos courtesy of AP Images unless otherwise indicated
Wolf's Words photos courtesy of Pittsburgh Steelers

To my father, Mehmet Ilkin, for having the courage to leave everything behind in Turkey and come to America. From this great man and very hard worker who was fearless, I learned so much about what it means to be a man.
                                                            —Tunch Ilkin

In memory of my Uncle Tom and in honor of my Uncle Will. They would have loved sitting with Tunch, as I did, and listening to his stories.
                                                            —Scott Brown

Contents

Introduction

A Thursday night game between the Pittsburgh Steelers and Tennessee Titans in 2017 reminded me why I love this game. It is because of the relationships.

That crisp November night at Heinz Field, I saw my ex-teammate and road roommate Mike Mularkey, who was head coach of the Titans. I saw my ex-teammate Keith Willis, who was an assistant defensive line coach for the Titans. I saw my ex-teammate Edmund Nelson, who is working for the NFL. I was with Craig Wolfley, my best friend and ex-teammate, as part of the Steelers' radio broadcast.

I also saw two of my ex-coaches, Tony Dungy, who was down on the field for NBC, and Dave McGinnis, an analyst for the Titans' radio broadcasts who was the defensive backs coach at Indiana State when I played there. Unlike the others, I ran into McGinnis, a former NFL head coach, in the press box. It was great seeing him and it was really similar to what had happened on the field when I saw the others.

I hadn't seen many of them for a very long time, but we picked up our relationship as if no time had elapsed. It was great talking to Keith and Edmund. We traded old war stories, reminisced about playing for Chuck Noll and how tough practices were. And we talked about battles. Keith and

I battled every day in practice—three times a week in full pads—like it was a game and we both brought out the best in each other. I can honestly say that games were easy after practicing against Keith. He made me the player I became because of the iron sharpening. Proverbs 27:17 says, "As iron sharpens iron, so shall one man sharpen another." Keith was that iron sharpener for me as a football player. The friendship that we developed because of that is still so close that we were hugging each other and telling each other that we love one another and that we really need to get together.

That is the essence of a football team. Something magical happens when you spend that much time with 45 guys—when you laugh together, when you cry together, when you win together, when you lose together, and when you bleed together. There is a bond that forms that is very hard if not impossible to separate. There is such a closeness that develops that you are friends forever. If you ask players who have retired what they miss most about the game, 99 out of 100 will tell you they miss the guys, they miss the relationships. That's what we had on the Pittsburgh Steelers in my 13 seasons with the team.

There is a book by Stu Weber, a pastor based in Oregon, called *Locking Arms*, and it's about male relationships. The ones who played in the NFL remember the Super Bowls and Pro Bowls, but they *talk* about the tough times, the battles. There is a depth to those relationships, a closeness that develops through the crucible of tough times and pressure.

Talking to Tony we were reminded how hard Chuck worked us and how so many coaches wouldn't have done that. I recalled a story by Dwain Painter, our wide receivers coach, who actually said to Chuck one day during the season: "You know, Coach, we're working them really hard. Don't you think we should go without pads one of these days, just to give them a break?" Chuck gave Painter that steely stare that could make you lose bladder control and said, "Do you ever watch the game of football?" Paint said, "Of course I do." Chuck said, "You noticed they play with pads, don't they?" That was the end of the conversation.

As I talked to Tony and Keith and Edmund and Wolf, we all laughed and told stories and it was just a great reunion, and that's what we called it: a reunion. Then I saw Mike, who became my roommate after Wolf left for Minnesota during free agency. I remember Mularkey was thinking about retiring and I talked him out of it. I said, "If you retire, who am I going to hang out with?" We always laugh because he had surgery after hurting his back that season and joke that it was because I made him come back. But we talked about old times as well, and I told him how much I admire him and the way he coaches. One thing Mike has always said is that Coach Noll had a tremendous influence on the way he coaches. Coach Noll had a tremendous influence on the way that Tony coached, too. Coach Noll has a tremendous influence on all of us in our lives so many years after we played for him. Each one of us recalled Chuck-isms, things that he used to say. Even when I see Steelers inside linebackers coach Jerry Olsavsky, another former teammate of mine, at practice we talk about what Chuck said—"Same foot, same shoulder, rising blow"—and on and on.

I ran into Dave in the press box dining room. He had retired after a long coaching career and was on a beach in California when the Titans called him and asked him to be the color man on their radio network. He was broadcasting just like I was, and we embraced and just kept going back to one another after the game to talk about old times, to renew old friendships, to talk about guys we had coached with and played with and how they were doing. It was a lovefest, it really was.

It may sound weird, but when you are in that kind of relationship, you develop a genuine love for one another. Coach McGinnis was one of the first guys who really believed in me when I was playing at Indiana State University. My senior year Dave said, "Tunch, my roommate at SMU was

Guy Morriss"—Guy had been the center for the Philadelphia Eagles for many, many years—"And Tunch, you're better than Guy Morriss was at this stage of your career and you'll do well in the National Football League." I remember thinking to myself, *Wow, he believes in me.* That kind of encouragement really spurred me on to be better than I thought I could be. Just seeing him that night, it was hard to say good-bye.

This book is ultimately about relationships. It's a book about locking arms. It's a book about teammates and the love they have for one another. And it's a book about football. In today's day and age with all of the controversy surrounding head injuries, it's almost like the NFL has become vilified. Let me tell you something: the NFL has been a great place to grow into manhood. I am thankful for every coach who I played for and every teammate I've ever had for the impact that they've had on my life.

I think we're trying to make it seem like football is evil. It's a physical, nasty sport, but it's had a huge impact on my life. I let my boys play and I'd have no problem with my grandsons playing. If I could have played for the money they make today, I would have liked that, but I loved playing in our era. It was much more fun. It was much more gladiatorial. It was much more intense. I loved the fact that what you did on a football field—if you did it on the street, you'd be thrown in jail. To me the intensity, the one-on-one battles, every day your manhood was challenged. I loved that. I think it helped me grow as a man. I loved my teammates. I loved my coaches. I also think that because there was no free agency in our day, we were closer because we were all together.

We couldn't afford houses all over the country, so we hung out together. Anything we did, we did together. Every Monday a group of us did something together. We rode dirt bikes or three-wheelers—Chuck would have had a conniption if he knew we were out riding—or went target shooting. We genuinely liked being with one another.

Again, you talk to ex-players and the thing they miss the most is the guys. They don't say, "Remember when we beat..." They say, "Remember that camp that Chuck killed us?" Wolf and I spend a lot of time at training camp because of our broadcasting duties, and before dinner we will sit on the hill that overlooks the fields at St. Vincent College. We will have a cigar and we will talk about old times, and it's mostly about the guys and the friendships.

CHAPTER 1

Chuck Noll

Chuck Noll was the consummate teacher. Every day with him was a lesson. Sometimes it was a lesson in X's and O's. Sometimes it was a lesson in technique. And sometimes it could be a lesson in history, vocabulary, or life in general. It was not unusual for Chuck to stop practice during team drills and address us by saying: "Understand what we're trying to do here. Don't just learn your position. Learn the entire offense. You don't have to be the biggest, strongest, or fastest guy to make plays. If you understand the game, you will put yourself into a position to make plays." That advice is something I heeded as a player and still follow as an analyst. It is part of what make Chuck one of the greatest coaches of all time. If you played for Chuck, you knew the game. I think that's why so many of his former players went into coaching or broadcasting.

The first time I met Chuck was before the 1980 NFL Draft when the Steelers brought three guys—Nate Johnson, Ted Walton, and me—in for physicals. I was just intimidated, awed and I wondered, *Is there really a chance I could get drafted here? They're the four-time Super Bowl champs. What would they want from an undersized guy from Indiana State?*

On the field, Chuck Noll coached us hard. Off the field, he was actually kind of a
Renaissance man.

The Steelers drafted me anyway, and my first encounter pretty much matched what it was like playing for Chuck—even after I had established myself. Noll could look at you and make you piss down your leg. You were just always uncomfortable around him because he was Chuck Noll and you had this image of him and you were trying to please him. Every time he looked at you, it was like he could see through you. He had that steely gaze, that stare, if you will, but he was a great coach, and I loved playing for him.

Our practices were brutal, and Chuck even had us cut block in practice, which is unheard of today. Training camp was a battle of attrition, and you figured they would back off once we got into the season. But we would be in full pads, and Chuck would be pushing buttons, and guys would be frothing at the mouth.

The thing about the game—it is one-upmanship. You win one, and I'm going to come back and win the next one. One day in my fourth season, Keith Gary and I were going at it, and it was a brutal practice. He would push me, and I would push him. One play he grabbed my facemask and he twisted it. I went ballistic. I was screaming, "I'm going to f'n kill you!" We were fighting and it got broken up, but I had snapped. Guys were trying to separate us, and all I saw was Gary over there and I was trying to get to him.

It seemed like the more guys that got in my way, the more my temper just went. I was going crazy and then I heard this voice, "All right, now I'm pissed off because you just punched me in the mouth." I looked at Chuck, and his lip was split. I said, "Oh. My. Goodness."

All of the sudden I went from a million miles an hour to *Uh oh. I'm gone.* Back then my wife, Sharon, and I lived in a townhouse complex in Bethel Park, and John Goodman, a defensive end, lived right across the street from us. John always beat me home from practice because I'd get in a lift and I had to watch a ton of film. A lot of times Sharon would see him coming and she'd ask him if he wanted to come to dinner because she always wanted to help people, and he was a bachelor. Here is the exchange that ensued after that practice:

Sharon: "J.R., do you want to come over for dinner?"
John: "I don't think so. I don't think you are going to be living there much longer."
Sharon: "What do you *mean*?"
John: "Tunch just hit Chuck. You guys are probably going to get cut."

Here is the conversation that took place after I got home:
Sharon: *"You punched Chuck?"*
Me: "I wasn't trying to!"
Sharon: "Did he come and talk to you after practice?"
Me: "No, he didn't say anything to me."
Sharon: "Oh my gosh, what do you think is going to happen?"
Me: "Honey, if I was going to get cut, I think they would have already done it. I don't think he's going to sit around and think about it."

I didn't get cut and played 12 seasons for Chuck, and, boy, was it a different relationship with him. One training camp we went to Carlisle, Pennsylvania, to practice against the Washington Redskins. We had a really good practice against them, and Chuck was in a really good mood. That night after practice they got a bunch of pizzas for all of the players, and Chuck was hanging out with the guys. Jon Kolb, who had become the strength coach, Mike Webster, Craig Wolfley, and I were having pizza and just drinking a beer with Chuck, who was really affable and very gracious. It was really this great time and it was almost like the first time I connected socially with Chuck. I think we all felt that way, and everybody was feeling really good about themselves.

Early the next day, we returned to camp in Latrobe, Pennsylvania. It was a long bus ride, and everyone was tired. Chuck said, "All right, go get your pads on. We're meeting out on the practice field in 20 minutes." I thought, *Where is the guy from last night?* Social Chuck was short-lived. All of the sudden, it was back to basics.

We lost to the Seattle Seahawks in the old Kingdome in 1981, and in the postgame team address, Chuck said, "We got outhit today. We've got to get back to basics." Normally the coaches have their own locker room and shower room, but for whatever reason, the coaches were showering with the players after that game. Wolf and I were in the shower, and he just started going off, saying: "Back to basics! Oh man, that is going to be miserable. It's going to be like camp. Back to basics? C'mon! We're eight weeks into the season! We don't need to be back to basics."

Chuck had a way of popping up when you least expected him to. Wolf, who didn't know Chuck was there, was lathering his hair and he kept going: "Back to basics. Back to basics." Wolf was facing me, and I started subtly shaking my head, trying to get him to stop. He was still saying "back to basics," when all of the sudden Wolf turned around and saw the coach who Steelers broadcaster Myron Cope had dubbed "Chaz the Emperor." Chuck just gave him this look and Wolf said, "Yeah, we've got to get back to basics this week."

Wolf's Words

We were in the locker room after the game, and Chuck was holding court with the media because they didn't have the press rooms like they do today. I heard a couple of clips, and with Coach Noll, you knew it was just going to be a horrible week to follow because he was speaking words that meant you were getting back to training camp and you were going to have loads of one-on-one drills, loads of hitting, loads of fighting, loads of conditioning. I was already disgruntled about the game. I was also disgruntled about having to fly all the way back to Pittsburgh. I was in the shower, sudsing up, and Tunch was off to my right and I was just going off. *Back to basics. Back to basics.* I was really honked off. I said, "Do you know how bad this is going to be? It's going to be horrible!" As I was doing this, I noticed that Tunch was trying to shake me off. He wasn't pointing at anything, but he was just giving me this look. He was trying to cut me off without being seen by someone else, but I wasn't getting it. I was just going on and on and on. I turned around and I gave one more, "Yeah, back to basics" and I looked, and Coach Noll was showering behind me. I looked at him, and he was looking at me with the eyebrows narrow and up on the end. It all came together with this fierce look. It just froze my heart. I said, "I think it's a great idea, Coach." That's all I could get out.

Chuck got me like that once, too. The day before a game against the Indianapolis Colts in 1984, we were at the Hoosier Dome having a light practice. Chuck was a tinkerer and he was looking at my stance. He said, "You know what? Your stance looks a little awkward. Let's try something." He made one of my feet more staggered than the other one. It felt awkward, and he said, "Try that." I tried it, and he said, "Try it again."

Chuck loved to practice at the visiting team's field the day before the game to familiarize yourself with the locker room and field and, as he said, to get the road trip out of your system, to get the flight out of your system.

I got on the bus after we had showered and I was sitting in about the fourth row, and defensive tackle Gary Dunn was sitting a row up across from me. I said, "Can you believe Chuck is messing with my stance?

He's got me changing my left hand. He's got me changing my right foot. Tomorrow I've got a couple of pretty darn good pass rushers—Donnell Thompson and Vernon Maxwell—and he's messing with me the day before the game!"

All of the sudden, Dunny started getting lower and lower in his seat. Right over him I saw Chuck. He turned around and looked at me and said, "I'm just trying to make you better. Do you want to get better?" I said, "Ah, yeah, Coach." Boy did I feel stupid.

I felt worse after an encounter with Maxwell the next day. He head-slapped me during one play, and I went crazy. We got into a fight, and he gave me the finger. I punched him in the face on the next pass rush, and he took a swing at me. I chased him down the field, yelling at him: "I'm going to get you! You're going to be wearing your ankle on your hip!"

Colts defensive tackle Leo Wisniewski, who is a buddy of mine and also a Christian brother—we've been in Bible study together—said, "Dang, Tunch, you better get that temper in check." The funny thing is that I later found out that the Colts were all rooting for me because Maxwell was not a very popular guy on their team.

Late in the game, we were leading by three points and driving, and Maxwell speared Frankie Pollard. I came flying in and I drilled him. I got the flag, and instead of first and goal on the 7-yard line, it was first and goal on the 22-yard line. We only ended up getting a field goal, and the Colts threw a Hail Mary after the kickoff. It ricocheted off four guys, and wide receiver Ray Butler caught it and sprinted into the end zone. We lost with the Colts scoring all of their points in the fourth quarter. We got into the locker room afterward, and Chuck said, "We've got one of our veterans, who should know better, starting a fight inside the 10. That makes no sense at all. Chuck didn't call me out by name, but everybody knew he was talking about me.

He was reaming me out. Then he paused and said, "I'm not trying to put this on one guy." I thought to myself, *Oh, no?* The guys are all ballbusters, so Gary Dunn and John Goodman said, "Hey, way to lose the game for us, Tunch." Then everybody started saying it jokingly.

I just remember how bad I felt, and later that season, it was almost déjà vu. We were playing the Denver Broncos in the playoffs, and Tommy Jackson speared Pollard. I went after Jackson and I nailed him. Flags went flying, and I thought they were on me. Tommy got up and said, "It was 62! Tunch, you should be out of the game, 62 out of the game, 62 out of the game!"

I thought, *Oh no! If I'm out of the game, I'm just walking right off the field right to the locker room and I'm going to take my own flight home. I am not going to go face Chuck.* Jackson was still going off, and I thought that I was out of the game. But he was flagged for the cheap shot, and they didn't flag me. I said, "Oh, thank you, Lord!"

Chuck didn't have a problem with one of the fights that I got into one game. Not surprisingly, Jerry Glanville was the head coach on the opposite sidelines that day—and the recipient of an infamous handshake. Our games with the Houston Oilers were always nasty—think Steelers-Bengals of recent years—and Glanville had his guys giving us cheap shots. Wolf and I retaliated, and a fight broke out. At the end of the game, Chuck was livid and he said to Oilers cornerback Steve Brown, "No. 24, tell your coach I'm going to meet him after the game and I'm going to kick his ass." Brown looked at him, and Noll said, "Who do you think is going to win?" Brown said, "My money's on you, Coach."

Chuck met Glanville at the end of the game and shook his hand and wouldn't let go. He was pointing, saying, "This shit's going to come back to haunt you." He was just going off on him. Wolf and I subsequently got fined—$500 for entering a fighting area and $500 for fighting. The next year we were playing a preseason game in New York, and we were appealing the fines. Chuck had brought the video, and Joe Browne of the NFL met with us. Chuck showed him the video and he said, "Listen, this is a bunch of crap. These guys were just defending their teammates. You know if you do not allow them to defend their teammates, you in essence emasculate them." Wolf looked at me and said, "Emasculate?" I said, "I'll tell you later." Chuck did this great presentation, like he was our attorney. I was like, *Wow, Chuck's in our corner!* We said, "We've got this locked." After hearing Chuck's defense Browne said, "Appeal denied."

Chuck's presentation and use of a 10-cent word offered a glimpse into something that was undeniable about the only coach to win four Super Bowls without losing one: he was much more than just a football coach. He was a wine connoisseur. He liked to cook. He flew airplanes. He loved classical music. He played the ukulele. *Who plays the ukulele?* One year the team brought the Pittsburgh Symphony Orchestra to training camp for a night, and Chuck was a guest conductor. It was crazy. I think they closed with "Stars and Stripes Forever." They said, "We have a special guest conductor. Would you come up here, Chuck Noll?" He really was a Renaissance man, something that came through in some of his speeches to the team.

After a Saturday practice before a game against the Raiders in Los Angeles, he said, "You know the Spartans were so committed to victory in 900 B.C. that when they sailed to the Corinth they burned their own boats. So, the only way they could return home was victorious on Corinthian ships. That's how committed we have to be."

Someone else joked, "Does that mean we're going to blow up our plane after we get to Oakland?" Someone else joked, "Corinthians? Spartans? What's he telling us college football stories for? This is the NFL." That's the way Noll was. His analogies and illustrations were deep.

Sharon saw a different relationship with Chuck one night when we were supposed to be out for a relaxing dinner. There was an Italian restaurant in Upper St. Clair—we lived right by it—and Chuck loved it. Sharon and I went there, and the maître d' said, "Your coach loves this place." I said, "That's what I hear."

A little later the maître d' came up to me and said, "Hey guess what? Your coach is coming." I looked around, and the place was packed. There was only one table, and it was right next to ours. I thought, *Oh, please don't put him there!* I was pulling out $20 bills just in case I needed to persuade someone to make other seating arrangements. Thankfully, the restaurant had a separate room, and I think it was a BYOB place. Chuck and Marianne, his wife, came, and they put them in the other room. I thought we were good, but as we were walking out, Marianne, who is very gracious, saw us. She said, "Tunch! Sharon! Come over here! Have a glass of wine!"

We went over to their table and Marianne and Sharon engaged in this conversation, and Chuck and I just sat there looking at each other. *So how was practice today? How's your elbow?* He was trying to make small talk. He was not ignoring me, but it was brutal. After three or four minutes, I said, "Oh, look what time it is! We've got to make a movie! C'mon, Sharon, let's go!" Sharon looked at me like, *What's gotten into you?*

We got outside, and Sharon said, "What was that all about?" I said, "*What was that all about?* I was sitting with Chuck! You were having this great conversation with Marianne. Guess what? My conversation with Chuck was not that great!"

She said, "You looked like a jack-in-the-box. You were so uncomfortable." I said, "I was. You play for him and see what it's like." It was an uncomfortable feeling because you were trying to please him and it was uncomfortable being in a one-on-one situation with him.

Wolf, like anyone who played for Chuck, knows about wanting to please him.

One season Wolf's groin was messed up. He had pulled it but kept sucking it up and practicing. He finally said, "I can't practice today. I'm just going to tell Chuck I can't go." I said, "Well, tell him." He said, "I've been starting for years. I should be able to take a day off. Look at it, it's black and blue. I've earned a day off." I said, "You go, boy. Tell Chuck that you're not practicing."

We were in the training room, and I was sitting right next to Wolf. Chuck walked in and said, "Wolf, how is the groin?" He said, "Great, Coach, I'm ready to go." Noll walked out, and everybody started cracking up. I said, "Boy, you told him. You folded up like a cheap card table."

Wolf's Words

I had pulled my groin, and my left leg was so swollen that it was two-and-a-half inches bigger than my right one and black and blue from my knee up to my hipbone. I had already practiced on Wednesday. We were on the table Thursday getting our ankles taped. I was looking at my leg, and it was just kind of throbbing. I was sitting there and I said, "You know? I think I'm going to take the day off." Tunch got this look on his face, and I should have seen it coming. When he poked the bear, he had this sort of look where the eyebrows got to be this unibrow from coming down together. He said, "Oh, really?" I said, "Hey, I've been a starter since '81. I see these young guys, and they take days off now. I think I need a day off, too." Tunch said, "Well, yeah. Sure, you could do that. I doubt you will." I said, "Oh, you don't think so?" At this point everybody started listening in the training room. Tunch said, "I dare ya. You're going to tell Chuck that you can't practice today?" I said, "Yeah, I'm taking the day off. We've got rookies here, and they're taking days off. I'm taking the day off." And now everybody was saying, "Ohhhh."

Tunch always did the thing from *The Christmas Story* where he went right to the triple-dog dare. He said that, and I puffed up and said, "You watch. I'm going to tell Chuck I need a day off." Not 10 seconds later, Chuck walked into the training room. If it happened today, I would say, "Okay, this is like MTV. You just got punked." That's how well choreographed this was. When Chuck walked in, everybody stopped and looked at him. He stopped right in front of the table where Tunch and I had our feet up because we were getting our ankles taped. He looked at me and said, "Hey, Wolf, how is the groin?" I looked right at him and I just panicked. I said, "I'm doing great, Chuck. I'm fine." I could just feel the heat and the redness coming up the back of my neck and into my face, and Chuck said, "Good. Let's have a good practice." The whole room just exploded, and Tunch just killed me. It was so bad. I should have known. Tunch started poking the bear and I went hook, line, and sinker.

One of the funniest things about Chuck was he really liked Bobby Kohrs, a linebacker who was in my draft class and played for the Steelers from 1980 to 1985. He always called him Robert. One day we were getting ready to go outside for a cold practice, and Chuck said, "Robert, make sure you're dressed accordingly. It's cold out there." He went outside and came back in and said, "Robert, are you wearing undergarments?" Kohrs didn't stand a chance.

We said, "What are you, Chuck's *son?*"

Later we were getting ready to leave for Seattle and we were going "Da-na-na-na…Da-na-na-na." I forget who started it, but we were in the locker room singing the theme song from *My Three Sons*. At our walkthrough in Seattle, the offense had finished and we were in the end zone. There were 10 of us lined up, and we started singing, "Da-na-na-na…Da-na-na-na."

We beat Seattle the next day, and everybody was feeling really good. Cliff Stoudt got on the plane microphone and started singing, "Da-na-na-na," and we all started doing it. Everyone was laughing, and the media that traveled on the team plane were trying to figure out what was going on.

Chuck asked Woody Widenhofer, our defensive coordinator, "What are they doing?"

He said, "They're saying that Bobby is your son, Chuck."

We later watched special teams film, and Kohrs made a nice play. Chuck said, "Nice job, Robert," and we started whistling the theme to *My Three Sons*. Chuck turned the projector off and said, "I'll tell you who's important around here: it's not the whistlers. It's the guys that get it done." That nipped it in the bud. There was no more *My Three Sons*, no more whistling. One of the trainers said jokingly, "You better be careful. Kohrs will get you cut around here."

I loved special teams and played it regularly until I became a starter in 1983. If you got an "atta boy" from Chuck during the special teams film session that was like getting high. I was running down on a kickoff one time and I blew up the wedge and made the tackle. Chuck went crazy and, as I came off the field, he said, "That's the way you blow up the wedge! That's the way you penetrate! That's the way you run down under kicks!"

During the film session he gave me the "atta boy." But on the next play I got blocked, and he said, "Tunch, don't rest on your laurels. By the way that was a little number that blocked you." That was a dig as he referred to wide receivers and other skill position players as "little numbers." One time I got blindsided and earholed and I hit the ground. He said, "The meek shall inherit the Earth." He had these great lines during film sessions.

We had a cornerback blocking the gunners, and the poor guy got beat like five or six times in a game. During the film session, Chuck said, "Look, you've got to get on this guy. You've got to move your feet." He was coaching him up, and the guy said, "Coach, that guy's 4.2." Chuck said, "What do you mean?" He said, "He's too fast." I said, "Uh oh. Wrong answer." And he was gone. Chuck could handle you not being able to get it done. But he could never handle you saying you couldn't get it done.

That may have ultimately led to Steve Courson, my good friend, getting traded in 1984. Steve was a phenomenal athlete, a really good guard, and a great fit among the offensive linemen. During his final season with the Steelers, we were watching game film, and Chuck was getting on Steve a little bit. Steve had a torn meniscus and he said, "Chuck, I'm playing on one leg. Maybe I shouldn't even be in there." I thought, *You don't ever tell Chuck you can't.* Chuck said, "Well, maybe you shouldn't." The next training camp Steve was traded to the Tampa Bay Buccaneers.

Dwain Painter, who was our wide receivers coach for many years, told me, "I learned more from Chuck than anybody else," and Paint had been around the NFL for a long time as well as at UCLA. We were talking about cuts one time at training camp, and he told me this story. He said the first cuts came around his first year with Chuck and he didn't know who to cut. Chuck told him that he had to cut three guys. Paint said, "Chuck, I don't know who to cut." Chuck said, "Well, first you cut the guys that can't. Then you cut the guys that won't." If you said you couldn't, in Chuck's eyes that meant you wouldn't.

Cheating is something else that Chuck wouldn't tolerate as I found out during the 1986 season. We played the Green Bay Packers at Three Rivers Stadium, and our defensive linemen said afterward, "Man, their jerseys were so slick." When you spray shoulder pads, people can't grab them, and one of the things defensive linemen like to do is grab the back of your jersey to pull you through on pass rushes. The Packers had left a bunch of empty cans of silicone spray in their locker room, and somebody suggested we try silicone. Everybody was spraying their shoulder pads with it. You didn't put on a lot to prevent it getting detected, and before the third game of our ill-fated silicone experiment, offensive tackle Ray Pinney was spraying his jersey, and I was next in line. Chuck came in and said, "What are you doing?" Ray said, "What's it look like I'm doing? I'm spraying my jersey."

Chuck said, "That's illegal. Putting a substance on your jersey is illegal. Plus, if it gets on the ball, if it gets on the hands of the quarterback, they're going to be dropping the ball. And we're the Pittsburgh Steelers. We don't have to cheat."

I walked into the locker room, and Chuck made a beeline for me. He said, "Do you do that?" I said, "No, sir, I don't do that." I was clean at the time, but I lied through my teeth. He told everybody about this in the locker room. That put an end to that.

Another thing Chuck didn't like was bodybuilding. Chuck *hated* any kind of bodybuilding, so when we did curls, we kept someone at the doorway of the weight room to make sure that if Chuck walked in, he would alert us. It didn't always work. One time we were doing curls and measuring our biceps, and Chuck said, "What are we doing, Tunch? Bodybuilding?" Another time we were doing curls and he said, "Ah, curls for the girls." And he walked out disgusted with us.

Chuck was about being functional. One time he got this idea that we could do this shuffle drill on the treadmill. We were doing this shuffle drill, pushing off as the treadmill was running, and he said, "Let me show you how to do it." As he was doing it, he said, "You can hop and switch." So just to set up the visual: he was sideways on the treadmill, and Terry Long and I were on one side, and Wolf was on the other side. When Chuck hopped to switch, he was facing the other side and lost his balance, and his feet got kicked out from under him by the treadmill.

As Terry, Wolf, and I watched, he hit the ground. It looked like a pop bottle rolling around on one of those old conveyor belts. We were almost crying from laughing, and Kolby was sitting in his office, which was all glass. He was eating an egg salad sandwich and nearly choking on his sandwich. Rolling around on the treadmill, Chuck jumped up and said, "But you can't get too cocky." Then he walked out. We all went into the training room and the locker room because we couldn't wait to tell the story. Terry said, "Man, I kind of felt sorry for him." I said, "I didn't." It was hilarious.

I can't say the same thing about our practices. They were so intense, and Chuck knew how to push buttons. He said things like, "If it was easy, everybody would do it. You've got to will your body." I don't know how many times he said, "We're going to cut back practice today," and practice went from two hours and 20 minutes to two-and-a-half hours. I would say, "I'm not a mathematical genius, but 2:20 to 2:30 is not cutting back."

One time at the end of practice, center Mike Webster had had enough and let Chuck know about it with a not so subtle gesture. Webby let a defensive player get upfield. He grabbed him by one of the buckles on the shoulder pads and then tossed him into Chuck, who said, "Okay, practice is over."

As great a coach as Chuck was in leading the Steelers to four Super Bowl victories in the 1970s, his best job may have come in the twilight of his career. We started 0–2 in 1989 after going 5–11 in '88. We lost 51–0 to the Cleveland Browns in Three Rivers Stadium and 41–10 the next week to the Cincinnati Bengals. Next up were the 2–0 Minnesota Vikings, who had looked unbeatable their first two games. The national media descended on Pittsburgh to write different variations of the same story: the game has passed Chuck by.

That Tuesday, Chuck said, "Smilin' Tunch. You're always smiling. I need you to be smiling today." I said, "Coach, I'll be smiling." He addressed the team later that day and said, "Be careful about what you let into your brain. Don't listen to the media. Treat them like mushrooms: keep them in the dark and feed them manure." He also said that week, "Your brain is like a swimming pool. You have water, you have acid, you have chlorine. If the ratio from cholesterol to sulphuric acid isn't just right you're going to..." He was losing us, so he got that Chuck look and said, "In other words don't let anybody piss in your pool." That was the mantra. We beat the Vikings 27–14, and that year we were a dropped ball from going to the AFC Championship Game.

Chuck coached two more seasons before retiring in 1991 and said something interesting when he got out of the game. He was interviewed about players in the 1990s and he said, "I'm not sure I could coach today's player." What he said after that was, "The problem with today's players is they evaluate themselves based on how much money they are making," and he was right. Chuck always said, "They can't pay you enough to play this game. You've got to want to play it for the love of the game." Now at playoff time, he would say, "Don't mess with my money," and we'd all laugh about that, but there is truth to what he said. You can't play the game for money.

He was also a celebrate-the-journey guy. I heard his son, Scott, and Marianne talk about this at the end of the season because Chuck would be down that the season—and the journey he loved—was over. He used to say the process is the purpose and he loved the process. Could he coach today? I don't know that he'd want to. Could he coach today if he started coaching today? Yes. Would he want to coach today after coaching when he did? That's a different question.

Chuck had a really good perspective, and his approach would seem anachronistic—look it up, Wolf—if not quaint in today's NFL and its around-the-clock coaching. The coaches' bad night with Chuck, as far as staying late, was Tuesday night. That was gameplan night, and they were there until 11:00. But you didn't have to be at work every night until 11:00, and Chuck used to say that you weren't going to discover something at midnight that was going to turn the tide of the game from a coaching standpoint. And it didn't matter what you knew if you couldn't get it across to your players. He was a master at that, and that's why he was a coach who transcended time and eras.

Your relationship with Chuck totally changed after you were finished playing for him. At least mine did. I interviewed him for FOX one night, and we just had a great time. After he retired from coaching, Wolf looked at me one time and said, "He looks smaller. He doesn't look as intimidating." I said, "That's because our future is no longer in his hands."

CHAPTER 2

Lessons from the 1970s Steelers

I said to someone after the Steelers drafted me in 1980, "If I make the team, I'm going to get at least one Super Bowl ring." Here I am almost four decades later and still without a ring. But it was such an honor to play with so many of the guys who helped the Steelers win four Super Bowls from 1974 to 1979. I learned so much from them—first and foremost how to be a professional just from their leadership. I wanted to be like Mike Webster. I wanted to be like Jon Kolb. I wanted to be like Larry Brown. I wanted to be like Joe Greene.

You probably start with Joe—at least from a playing standpoint—when talking about that Steelers dynasty because he was such a dominant force. Early in his career, he was the wild and wooly cowboy and then he was the king during the prime of his career. Then at the end of his career, he was the one who dripped of wisdom, the old sage. In every one of those phases of his career, he had an impact on those around him. He made everyone around him better. There was something about Joe and his presence that you wanted him to think you were good. You wanted him to respect you, so you worked really hard.

There's an integrity to playing the game. You want to be a hard worker, you want to be dependable, you want to show up. But you want certain people to see this you more than others, and Joe was one of those guys. Chuck Noll was one of those guys. It's funny because Joe in many ways was like Chuck. Defensive back J.T. Thomas said that Noll drafted guys to reflect his personality, and Chuck always said, "If I have to fire you up, you're in the wrong business. I want guys that are already fired up."

I saw how fired up Joe could get plenty of times. One of those moments stands out, and it happened early in my career. We lost two games in a row in 1981, and Joe called a players' only meeting the night before we played the Falcons in Atlanta. I had never been to a players-only meeting, and Joe stood up in the hotel room and said, "I don't know what's wrong with us, but we need to fix it. We're not taking the field like we used to. When we used to take the field, *we took the field*. We've got to get back to that. We've got to get back to taking care of the details. We have to get back to where we were—and we are going to start tomorrow." I had never seen that before. The room was completely quiet, and we won the following day 34–20.

Joe had a way of making us speechless even after he was no longer playing. He joined Chuck's staff as a defensive line coach in 1987. When we were doing one-on-one drills against the defensive linemen, he got so pissed off that he once kicked the ball into the end zone. He then walked into the stands, sat in a seat, and just stayed there. We stood there like, *What are we supposed to do now?* Meanwhile, I thought, *What is he going to do? I hope he doesn't go in and put the pads on.*

Even as a coach, Joe had that intensity where you were never quite sure what was going on behind those eyes. The funny thing is he's such a teddy bear now. He's so loving and nice. We were on a Steelers cruise

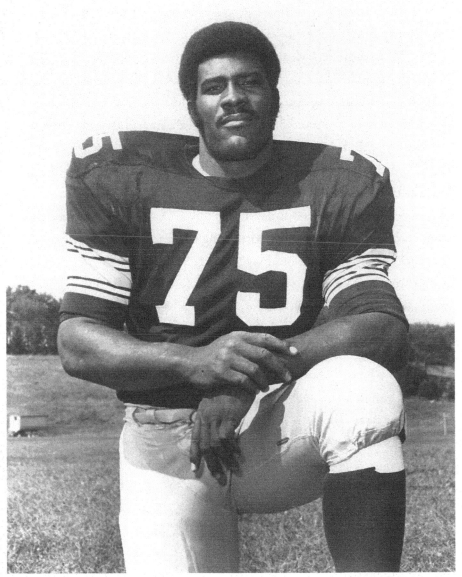

When you talk about the Steelers' dynasty, you have to start with Joe Greene.

together in 2017, and they showed video of him elbowing two guys from the Philadelphia Eagles and punching Denver Broncos guard Paul Howard, and he said, "Oh, I was just misunderstood." He was just downplaying it, but when Rocky Bleier spoke, he said, "That's crap. You were mean." Joe doesn't like the Mean moniker. Mean Joe Greene is gone. I never realized that he, too, was intimidated to a certain extent by Chuck. We were sitting around when Joe was coaching for the Arizona Cardinals, and I said, "Joe, did Chuck intimidate you too?" He said, "Oh, yeah, he had that effect on me."

The dynamic between Chuck, and Terry Bradshaw was interesting to watch, and this was after Terry had established himself as an all-time great and four-time Super Bowl winner. Early in my career, I stood next to Chuck on the sidelines so that he knew I was alive. One of the funniest things about standing beside him was witnessing his reactions when Terry would drop back to pass. Chuck would say, "No, Terry, no, no, no! Safety! Safety… Good throw, good throw, good throw!" Or Terry would drop back to pass, and Noll would say, "Watch the flat, Terry, watch the flat! No, no, no, no… Good throw, good throw, good throw, good throw!"

Terry had so much confidence in his arm and he always believed he could put it where he wanted it. When Chuck wondered what he was thinking, Terry would just respond, "Gee, Chuck, I just thought Swannie would go up and get it." That was his response half the time. To him it was fun. *C'mon, let's beat these guys and have some fun. Give me some time so I can throw deep and have some fun.* Terry was one of the most confident athletes I have ever seen. I only played four years with him and I only played in a couple of games where he was actually at quarterback so I don't have some of the rich Terry stories that some of the guys do, but he was just a great guy. He made you feel like you were part of it. He didn't make you feel like you were a rookie. He busted your balls and said, "C'mon, rook," but he didn't really make you feel like a rookie.

Terry was a leader in the way the provided encouragement. He wasn't the one who was going to say, "Hey guys, we've got to take care of business." That was Joe's role. That was Jack Lambert's role. That was Webby's role. People always ask me, "What was Terry like?" What you see is what you get. I never saw the other side of Terry, the bitter side of Terry that you often hear about.

I also played four years with Franco Harris, and Franco really cared about the team. After the San Diego Chargers playoff loss in 1982, he and his wife, Dana, took everybody out to dinner, and we just talked about the season. Franco was always doing nice things for his teammates like hosting dinners, getting us all together. That continued even after his playing days were over. He hosted a dinner for a bunch of us, who are still in the Pittsburgh area, and gave us small statues with our names on them. That was Franco. He loved his teammates and never stopped thinking about them. He thanked everyone who ever blocked for him in his Pro Football Hall of Fame acceptance speech.

Franco had unbelievable vision. One of the things that made him so great was his ability to stop and start. He had a great feel for the trapping game that we ran and he had patience like Le'Veon Bell, though not quite to that degree, but he also knew when he had to hit the hole quick. He was big and he was elusive at the same time.

Franco is so big that the first time I saw him, I thought, *What a beast.* And he was really such a nice guy. When I first met him, he said, "Hey, Tunch how are you doing? Nice to meet you. Welcome to the Steelers." In 1982 we played the Cleveland Browns, and he had a big game and got a lot of his yardage on backside cuts where I was. He said, "Tunch, you just keep doing that. Way to open it up, way to open it up!" He gave such encouragement the whole game. I would hear stories about other teams, about in-fighting and jealousy, and I never experienced that with the Steelers. I always felt guys were in my corner, and they were just great, great guys.

John Stallworth and Lynn Swann were grace and poetry in motion. The game was different at that time. It was a more run-first game, but those guys brought big plays. Stallworth made a catch in 1984 against the Kansas City Chiefs when he was falling down, tipped the ball up, and then tipped it to himself. I think I was blocking Art Still, and we both just stopped, looked at each other, and said, "Did you see that?" Swannie and Stallworth made catches that made you just go, "Wow." And they were both tougher than they were given credit for. They were just fun to watch.

There are a handful of Pro Football Hall of Famers from that era on the defensive side of the ball, too, and when people think of Jack, they think of the intensity, and, boy, was he intense. They think of the nastiness, and, boy, was he nasty. And he was a really good player. The really good inside linebackers read the play so fast that they beat you to the spot, and that's what made Jack so good. He beat you to the spot, and you couldn't get a hat on him. That's why he had so many tackles. He was such a smart player and he was such a great tackler. He had this sixth sense of knowing where the ball was and Jack was never out of position. He studied a lot of film and took a no-nonsense approach to that as he did most things.

Woody Widenhofer, our former defensive coordinator, tells a story about Lambert coming to Pittsburgh after the NFL draft his rookie year and wanting to watch film. Some sort of media reception was going on at Three Rivers Stadium, and Widenhofer said, "Do you want a hot dog?" Lambert said, "I didn't come here to eat hot dogs. I came here to study film."

During my second year with the Steelers, New Orleans Saints quarterback Archie Manning told me a great story about Lambert. Billy Hurley was playing for the Saints, and we played them in New Orleans, so I stayed there after we beat the Saints on Sunday because we had Monday off. Billy and I had been roommates the year before, and I wanted to hang out with Billy and spend some time in New Orleans. The next day Billy had to go in for treatment on his knee, and I was in the Saints locker room with him. Manning walked in, and Billy introduced us, and we talked about the game. The first thing Archie said to me was, "Boy, that Lambert is crazy." I said, "Yeah, I know." He said, "You know that play-action pass that I threw over his head for like 20 yards? Well, he jumped on the play-fake. We had been running that off-tackle play with Chuck Muncie so much that he was just waiting for it. I'm running down the field after the completion, and Lambert's yelling at me, 'That's chicken shit, Manning! That's chicken shit!' I thought he was going to hit me because I faked him out. I just thought it was a great call." That was just Lambert.

I only played with Jack Ham for a couple of seasons, but I will say this: he played angles better than any outside linebacker I ever tried to block. We had this play called *16 U* where the tight end came down on the defensive end and the right tackle kicked out against the outside linebacker. The first time I ran it against Ham I thought I had the angle on him. He dipped his shoulder and sliced in between me and the tight end to blow up the running back.

It was like he went from visible to invisible. That was how quickly he beat me, and I went back to the huddle, looked at Larry Brown, and said, "How did he do that?" He said, "You've got to keep your eye on Hammer." It just happened so fast. He had this knack for knifing his body so you couldn't get a hit on him. And if you tried to play soft on him, he drilled you.

Mel Blount also drilled you, even though he was known more for his blanket coverage as a cornerback. Mel was 6'4", 215 pounds—bigger than Lambert—and just a freak of nature. Against the New York Giants in our first preseason game in 1981, there was a quick out to a wide receiver. The guy caught the ball, and Mel picked him up, hip tossed him, and drove him on his head. He completely ragdolled him, and I just said, "Oh, man, first preseason game!" Mel could have just pushed him out of the bounds, but he was proving a point.

J. T. Thomas tells the story that no matter what the defense was, Mel was always playing man-press coverage. It didn't matter if it was Cover 2, Cover 3, whatever. He had those long arms and could give you a wedgie from across the locker room. When he jammed a guy, it was like deceleration trauma. The receiver would just stop and couldn't move. Mel also had the speed and athleticism to turn and run with you. They changed the rules because of him.

Even today Mel is almost regal. When Mel walks into a room or onto the practice field, everybody stops and turns their head. It doesn't matter what other Hall of Famer is in that room. But he is such a great guy, such a good man, such a godly person. He has made such an impact through the Mel Blount Youth Leadership Initiative. He still wears that cowboy hat, and a lot of guys shave their heads today, but I think Mel was one of the first to do it. Someone asked him once why he shaved his head. He said, "Because if I can't have all of my hair, I don't want any of it."

Not only was he a great teammate, but he also had this genuine concern for you. Even today when I see him, he has such an affirming nature. Just like Franco, he provided such encouragement, and I am better off having played with him and I am better off having him as a friend. He wanted to make you a better football player and a better man.

There should be more players from those Steelers teams in the Pro Football Hall of Fame, and it is a terrible injustice that Donnie Shell, L.C. Greenwood, and Andy Russell aren't in it. I understand why there is an anti-Steelers sentiment in the Hall of Fame because they feel that too many Steelers are already in, but Andy was going to Pro Bowls when they stunk.

It's a lot harder to go to the Pro Bowl when your team is struggling. He should be in the Hall of Fame.

The same goes for L.C. He was tall and skinny and couldn't lift a lot of weight, but, boy, could he play and he'd headbutt you. He looked more like a basketball player than a football player, but he had this way of turning his body sideways so you wouldn't get much to hit. We called him "the Cape" because he was like a matador. The recurring line for L.C. was, "Oh, he gave him the cape." L.C. was a great guy and just funny. During practice he often knew the offense was snapping the ball on the first sound and he would say, "Blue" because that was one of the color codes. Every time I jumped offside, he would kind of chuckle. He had that deep baritone laugh. But he would also impart wisdom and say, "Stay off the streets at night, rook. Get your rest."

A lot of players wished Donnie Shell had rested more on the field. Donnie had more interceptions than any strong safety in NFL history. He played like a human torpedo. One time in training camp, Craig Wolfley pulled out on a sweep and he thought he was going to lock up Donnie, but Donnie came up and just blew him up. Wolf came back to the huddle and said, "Big hitter, Shell." Greg Hawthorne thought Donnie was going a little too hard in one practice and said something to him. Donnie said, "Well, Greg, if you're going to surrender, just drop your drawers and throw up the white flag."

Donnie had this way of knocking you out and then telling you that Jesus loves you. He lived his life for Jesus and he played football for Jesus. People asked him, "Mr. Shell, you play a violent game. How do you reconcile that with your faith in Christ?" He always said, "Easy. God gave me this talent to play in the National Football League. In return I am giving him all of me, and the intensity that I play with is just utilizing the gift that He gave

41

me and giving glory to Him." And he was right because there was never a game where he didn't give glory to God.

He was a great teammate except sometimes he got guys with friendly fire because he hit everything that moved. The other thing that made Donnie so great was he was such a smart player. He was always in position to make a play. Whenever there was a fumble, it seemed like he was there. If a ball was tipped, he was always there. He had a knack for always being in the right place at the right time. He and Troy Polamalu were similar, but Troy freelanced a lot more.

Donnie was the quintessential guy Chuck talked about when he said you didn't have to be the biggest, strongest, or fastest guy to make plays. Donnie understood the game so well and saw plays develop. Guys who play in the middle of the field—safety and inside linebackers—the really great ones play with their eyes, and that's what Donnie did. Did he have a high football IQ? Absolutely. Did he study a lot of film? Without a doubt. He was a great teammate and just a sweetheart of a guy.

Donnie was the biggest hitter I've ever seen at safety. That's exemplified by what he did to Houston Oilers running back Earl Campbell in the AFC Championship Game. Campbell had a bunch of yards in the first half, but the game basically ended when Donnie hit Campbell. And Donnie, of course, wanted to pray for Campbell.

Defensive lineman Gary Dunn was another guy who never got the credit he deserved because he was on that Steelers defense with so many big names. He had a great swim move. He would shake on you and swim, but he could also run over you. He played one game with cracked ribs against New England Patriots guard John Hannah and he had a great game against the Hall of Famer. George Perles, our defensive line coach, said after the game, "Dunny, with those broke ribs, man he did a number on John Hannah, all-world John Hannah! He's the nucleus of our defense! Heck, he's the nucleus of our team!" Gary had a number of nicknames, including "Fat Albert" and "Disco" because he loved to disco dance, but we started calling him "Nuke" after that game.

Linebacker Bryan Hinkle was like Hammer. He might not have been as gifted, but he never got hooked, was never out of position. He was a very smart player and a great complement to Mike Merriweather and Greg Lloyd because he was so steady. Hink allowed Merriweather and Lloyd off the other side to be more of freelance guys, more of pass rushers. We joked that Hink was always miserable. His locker was next to mine, and we played 12 years together. Every day in practice, he said, "I've had enough of this shit. I'm retiring. I can't do this anymore." I always said, "You love this game." We always said that he's not happy unless he's miserable.

Another linebacker, David Little, was also a terrific player. He was smart, physical, and tough. He went about his business very professionally and was a real good locker room guy. My second season was his rookie year, and we were really competitive on special teams. We developed a friendly competition and we always helped each other. We tried to make each other better. My heart was broken when he passed away in 2005 at the young age of 46.

Lloyd and I battled all of the time later in my career and he is every bit as competitive as I am. When we battled it was always at game speed because there was no holding back. He wanted to win, and I wanted to win. We talked trash to one another, and he was one of those guys who made you better from practicing against him. We took plays off against different guys but never against each other. After he made first Pro Bowl in 1992, he came back to Pittsburgh, and I had not seen him very much that offseason. I went to a Pittsburgh Pirates game and saw him wearing a Pro Bowl T-shirt, a Pro Bowl hat, and Pro Bowl shorts. I sarcastically asked, "Hey, Greg, did you make the Pro Bowl this year?" I had to bust his chops. He laughed and said, "Yeah, we got some really cool stuff." I said, "Yeah, I can tell."

Man, was he usually serious, though, and Jerry Glanville once called him "the meanest man in the National Football League." He played like it.

Running back Frankie Pollard was tougher than a woodpecker's beak. He ran between the tackles hard, picked up the blitz. He lit you up and then had a big smile on his face—a lot like Hines Ward in that way. He was very physical and wouldn't back down from anybody. You loved playing with Frankie. He was underrated and underappreciated.

Defensive back Rod Woodson was probably the most athletic football player I've ever seen. He used to catch the ball over his head on kickoff returns and punt returns. Chuck loved that about him, and I never understood why. I think he meant that when you catch it over your head you catch it with your hands more. Chuck would always say, "That's the way you catch the ball."

During his rookie year, Rod overslept one time and was late for a Saturday practice. Everyone was saying, "Where's Rod?" Wolf, Dunny, and I saw him come out onto the field and we said, "Get him, Chuck! This is going to be great!" What did Noll do? He put his arm around Rod like a father, like he was telling him it was okay. We said, "That's not what we expected."

Defensive lineman Keith Willis was a great player and he is still tied for third on the Steelers' list for most sacks in a season with 14. We really went at it in practice, and when I saw him before the Tennessee Titans-Steelers game in 2017, I said, "Hey, do you remember when you kicked me in the balls?" He said, "That was not me. That was the other Keith Willis." I said, "No, I remember very distinctly that you kicked me in the balls." We had been swinging at each other, and he just snapped. The funny thing about Keith and I is we never took our battles off the field. We prayed together and were in Bible study together. We had this very close relationship, and I nicknamed him "Skippy." One day he showed up for practice wearing cuffed corduroys, saddle shoes, and an argyle sweater. I said, "Oh my goodness, when did you get the preppy look? We're going to start calling you 'Skippy.'" The name stuck.

On a sad note Gabe Rivera could have been—maybe not the next Joe Greene but—something special. When Gabe headbutted you, your body felt like a tuning fork. You felt it down to your toes. I remember the night when his tragic car accident happened. It was a Friday night before the Tampa Bay Buccaneers game, and I was watching the news when they reported the accident. A policeman came in to see us afterward and said, "Do you know that if Gabe was wearing a seat belt, the worst thing that would have happened to him is he might have broken both legs." Now he is a paraplegic, and that was when I started wearing my seatbelt.

Steelers Pro Bowlers

Andy Russell is one of only 10 players who made at least seven Pro Bowls while with the Steelers. He and Alan Faneca are the only ones who are eligible for the Pro Football Hall of Fame who haven't been inducted. Faneca was a finalist for the Hall of Fame in 2017 and 2018 and is expected to gain admission.

The Steelers who have been to the most Pro Bowls:

Name	# of Pro Bowls
Joe Greene	10
Franco Harris	9
Jack Lambert	9

Ernie Stautner	9
Mike Webster	9
Jack Ham	8
Troy Polamalu	8
Dermontti Dawson	7
Alan Faneca	7
Andy Russell	7
Rod Woodson	7

CHAPTER 3

Mike Tomlin

I do not understand why so many Steelers fans want to take shots at Mike Tomlin. He is a great coach and a great man. He loves the game, he loves the Steelers, he loves his players, and he loves this community. I mean he really loves Pittsburgh. I love the way he coaches, and in many ways, he is like Chuck Noll, a consummate teacher.

He is so engaged during practice and he makes sure everyone else is, too. A lot of times I'll stand next to him at practice just to hear him coach and I learn something from him every day. He often asks the players who aren't on the field at the time: "What were you thinking? What was the call?" One of the things he says to the young players on the sidelines is, "As you watch the defensive backs make the call on the sidelines, make the call to yourselves so you understand." He's always asking them questions on the sidelines and wants to make sure that they're all paying attention at the same time. He places an emphasis on communication.

He coaches all aspects of the game, too, and no detail is too small. I heard him tell the offense, "Remember, on interceptions all defensive backs are cutback runners. They see color and they cut back so make sure you get after it." Other coaching tips he uses are, "Let the down and distance talk to you" and "If you have a bad play, go on to the next play. Don't be paralyzed by the mistake you just made. Don't carry that luggage with you." I love too that no matter what goes on, he says, "There's no panic here. There's no throwing up the white flag."

He told cornerback Artie Burns, "How is your independent study going?" That was his way of saying to the young cornerback: you better be studying; don't just come and learn in meetings and in practice. You've got to be doing your due diligence. He always talks about being accountable to one another, and that's a big part of his message to his players. You're not just playing for yourself; you're playing for the guy next to you.

People think that he is not a disciplinarian. That is the biggest bunch of bullcrap I've ever heard. He holds these guys accountable and he knows how to poke the bear. He knows exactly how to motivate. He knows when to yell, when to needle, and when to bust your chops. Herm Edwards said, "I don't coach everybody the same way. I don't treat everybody the same way. But I treat everyone fair." That's the way Tomlin is. He's not going to treat Cameron Heyward the same way he treats Javon Hargrave. Cam has earned his spurs, and so Mike is going to treat him differently than he treats a young player. He knows who to come down on, who to coddle, and who to encourage.

One of the things the Steelers allow me to do is go into the scouts' room to watch film. A lot of times, I'll get there early in the morning. Before he got hurt in 2017, Ryan Shazier was always there with Mike Mitchell and Vince Williams. At different times Sean Davis or Tyler Matakevich would frequent the scouts' room for viewings. Most days Mike walked in and watched with us. He offered pointers on how we should watch film and said things like, "Don't let the film paralyze you. Let the volume of the film give you reference points." In other words, a lot of time people get paralyzed

Head coach Mike Tomlin displays his intensity during a *Monday Night Football* game in 2017, but he also cares deeply about his players.

by going back and forth, back and forth, and I am guilty of that. He means that you shouldn't get bogged down on one play. He says, "Let the film roll. Repetition is the key. Make sure you let the totality of the film wash over you." What a great coaching point. That way you pick up on tendencies, personnel groupings, and a number of things that jump out.

When Mike took over for Bill Cowher in 2007, my first impression of him was, "Wow, is he young." That was more of an indictment of me than it was of him, and immediately I was very impressed with him. Right from the get-go, you could see his passion for the game, and at one of his early press conferences, he said that everybody kept asking him what the players thought of him. He said it didn't matter what the players thought of him. It mattered what he thought of them. I thought to myself, *Now, that's old school.* He wasn't concerned how they perceived him. I was in the room when he said that before Super Bowl XLIII, too.

He has a maturity and wisdom beyond his years, and you saw it in how he dealt with the question of whether he would keep the 3-4 defense the Steelers had been running under Dick LeBeau or switch to the defense he had been running with the Minnesota Vikings. I loved it when he said, "Why would I get rid of one of the greatest defensive minds ever?" As good of a defensive coordinator as he was running a 4-3, Tampa 2 defense, he said, "I'm going with Dick." He was totally secure with himself.

Good coaches will take input, and Chuck was like that. When we beat the Houston Oilers in the wild-card round of the playoffs in 1989, Rod Woodson forced Lorenzo White to fumble in overtime, but then we went three-and-out. Chuck sent the punt team out. Rod Rust, the defensive coordinator, called from up in the press box and said, "Chuck, I don't think we're going to be able to stop them again." Chuck called timeout and sent out Gary Anderson. He made a 51-yard field goal, and we won the game. The fact that Rod felt confident enough to tell Chuck that the defense was gassed and that Chuck was secure enough in Rod's judgement is an example of how coaching is a collaboration and you've got to let your coaches coach. I really admire that about Mike. He lets his coaches coach like Chuck did.

One of the things that I also admire about Mike is he cares deeply about the development of his players as men, fathers, and especially mentors. We do this event every year together called, ManUp Pittsburgh. It basically challenges dads to be the father God called us to be and to father the fatherless, to get a protege. He had mentors in his life and he talks about his stepdad and granddad and the impact they had upon him. I have a mentee, Tony, that I have been mentoring for more than five years now. After about three years with him, there was a time when Tony didn't want to spend any time with me. I called and showed up at his house, and he just blew me off. I thought he didn't want anything to do with me and I just figured, *Okay, I guess this thing has run its course.*

At the ManUp Pittsburgh event in 2017, Mike talked about his relationship with his stepdad and how the helping hand of his stepdad, who really tried to help him, was made more difficult by Mike. The coach said, "So listen, don't get discouraged if these guys don't make it easy on you. Stay after them." I left ManUp and the first thing I did was call Tony's mother. I said, "I miss Tony. How's he doing?" She said, "Oh, Tunch, he's going through some hard times. His best friend got killed in a drug deal. One of his other good friends got sent to prison. The Lord is working on him." I said, "Do you think he wants to see me?" She said, "Oh, he loves you. It's just that he was feeling shame." I said, "Well, I want to see him again."

He and I picked right back up where we left off, and I see him once a week. I told Mike, "I've got to tell you: you inspired me to call Tony." I told him the story, and he was just so pleased about that. He said, "Well, I'd love to meet him." I said, "How about I bring him to practice or camp?" We were on the practice field one day, and Tony was with me. Mike was on the other side of the field and he walked all the way over probably about 50 yards and said, "Is this Tony?" I said, "Yes, it is." He met Tony and started carrying on a conversation with him. I brought Tony back to practice about two weeks later, and he saw us and said, "Tony! What's happening, buddy? Come on over here. It's great to see you."

Mike wants to help others. He wants to help at-risk kids. He wants to help people who are less fortunate. When he talked to Ed Glover of Urban Impact, he said, "We've got to help Tony. We've got to help people like Tony." I just think that is so great that he recognizes that need in our community.

He also wants to be part of this organization called Operation Underground Railroad. It is made up of former CIA operatives and Navy Seals who try to take back young girls who have been captured and put in bondage. Mike saw a documentary on the sex slave trade and said, "We've got to do something. We live in a very divisive world, but everyone can get behind this." That's how he and the Steelers became involved with Operation Underground Railroad.

He is so conscientious of what's going on in the community and Mike never forgets his roots. Craig Wolfley and I were doing our radio show at the commissary at the Reserve Center out by the old airport and we were celebrating Veterans Day in 2017. We asked if we could interview a couple of soldiers, and one of the guys we interviewed was LaMarri Williams, who happened to have played high school football with Mike in Newport News, Virginia. He talked about what a great guy Mike is and said, "We always knew Mike was going to be a head coach. He just had that leadership." What people don't realize is Mike is brilliant. He went to William & Mary and was on his way to becoming an attorney. As a matter of fact, his parents were really disappointed when he said, "I'm going to coach instead of become a lawyer."

Williams' mother was an English teacher at the grade school they attended. Mike is so articulate and has such a command of the English language that she always jokes that she taught him that. When I saw Mike the day after the Thursday night win against the Tennessee Titans in early November, I said, "Hey, I know now why you are so articulate and have such a command of the English language." He said, "Ohhh?" I said, "Yeah, your grade school English teacher, Mrs. Williams."

He said, "How do you know Mrs. Williams?" I told him the story, and he said, "Can you get me LaMarri's phone number? I want to call him." We got him the phone number, and he called him right away. That was very cool. I've learned a lot from Mike about the game and about life. I appreciate his willingness to put his heart out there.

Mike endured another round of heavy criticism after the Steelers lost to the Jacksonville Jaguars 45–42 in the divisional round of the 2017 playoffs, and I thought it was way off base. The Steelers lost because they didn't execute. I didn't see Mike miss one tackle. I didn't see him miss one block. It's on the players. Make the plays. Execute. It's not like the coaches weren't putting them in position to make plays. The defense simply wasn't good enough. Ask any one of them, and each player will tell you that. How come people weren't criticizing Bill Belichick for the way his defense played in the ensuing Super Bowl? And Philadelphia Eagles coach Doug Pederson is a genius because he went for it twice on fourth down in the Super Bowl? If those plays didn't work, is he a genius? No, it would have been, *Why would you try a double-reverse pass on the 1-yard line?* It kills me that that people make these blanket statements, especially ones suggesting Mike doesn't instill discipline.

I love when media guys, especially talk-show hosts, say, "Well, this is what I would have done." Well, you know what? I'm sorry, but you haven't been in that position. I also love when a media guys says, "Oh, I watch the film." Really? Do you really know how to watch film? Do you know what to look for? Can you spot combination coverages, which every team does most of the time? You don't always know who broke down in the blocking scheme. Sometimes it's obvious; sometimes it's not. Second-guessing has become a way of life, and not everyone knows what they're talking about. Pro Football Focus? Give me a break. Who are the guys doing the evaluating? Have they ever put a jockstrap on? Just because you can play *Madden NFL* and you know there's Cover 1, Cover 2, Cover 3, Cover 4 defense doesn't make you the next Buddy Ryan.

Terry Bradshaw, my former teammate, seems to go out of his way to take shots at the Steelers. I love Terry, but he was wrong when he said Mike was a "great cheerleader" instead of a great coach. Terry's never here, so how does he know? I think it's just unfair of him. I'm a huge Mike fan.

Mike has been to two Super Bowls, and I know everybody wants to say, "Well Belichick…" Okay, I'll give you that. He's not Belichick, but Belichick is the best coach in the NFL. Now who's the second best? We've got a guy who is right up there. I'm all for that. Pederson is going to be the hot coach now because he won a Super Bowl and he beat Belichick, and you do have to love that. He's a great coach who loves his guys, but he's not old school. He's more like Mike, who loves his guys and is a player's coach. There's only one old-school coach in the NFL, and that's Belichick.

Mike doesn't get enough credit. But that doesn't bother him. He doesn't need his ego fed. He doesn't need a pat on the back. He doesn't need affirmation from the media or the public. He's more concerned with the people in the room. He's very secure in who he is and he knows that if you try to please the people outside the room you're going to end up getting fired anyway.

Chuck was the same way. Mike has the same steely resolve that Chuck did. It manifests itself in a different way; maybe Mike is more demonstrative, but it's the same thing.

I remember when Mike Mularkey was the head coach of the Buffalo Bills, and they started one season 0–3. Everyone was screaming to change the quarterback, change the offense, change this, change that. He said, "We're not going to change anything." That goes back to Chuck's influence. Chuck always said, "Change for the purpose of change is no change at all. We're going to stick with what we know works." Mike is like that, too, and I think there is real wisdom in that. Now, when you need to make a change, you make it. But you don't make it for the sake of making a change.

There are so many similarities between Mike and Chuck. They have different styles but the same philosophy. Mike wants smart football players; Chuck wanted smart football players. Mike will stop practice to make a point; Chuck stopped practice to make a point. Chuck always said, "Understand what we're trying to do here; understand what they're trying to do to us." Tomlin is more of a "make-sure-you-see-it" type coach. It's different terminology, but it's the same general thing. They both wanted you to understand the game.

Rocky Bleier tells this great story about Chuck and holding onto the past. There are two monks traveling through a forest, and they come to a brook, and there's a lady there by herself. She can't get across so one monk picks her up and carries her across. She thanks him, and they proceed on for a while. The monk who didn't carry the girl or have any interaction says to the other monk, "You know it's forbidden for us to have any contact with the opposite sex. Yet you carried her across the brook." The other monk looks at him and says, "Yes, I just carried her across the brook, but you carried her all the way here."

Chuck told that story after a bad loss and then said, "Dismissed. I'll see you tomorrow." The moral of the story is—and what Mike would say—don't get paralyzed by your mistake. Don't carry that baggage with you. Chuck always said, "Whatever it takes." Mike says, "The standard is the standard." It is different wording, but it's the same message. High standards remain intact with the Pittsburgh Steelers.

CHAPTER 4

The 2017 Season

The Steelers went 13–3 and won the AFC Central, but their season met a disappointing end when they lost to the Jacksonville Jaguars in the divisional round of the playoffs. Coaching was not the reason why the Steelers lost that game. Former NFL head coach Mike Nolan told me this statistic while at a coaching clinic: if you get a return for a touchdown in a game, you win at least 75 percent of the time. I'm not a big stat guy, but that was very insightful. The Jaguars had three returns for touchdowns against the Steelers in two games in 2017, and you can't win that way. When you give up those kinds of plays, it kills you.

Plus, they beat us physically and played like a team that had Tom Coughlin's imprint on it. When Coughlin took over the expansion-team Jaguars as head coach, his goal was to build a tough football team to compete with the Steelers because both teams were in the AFC Central at the time. They built the same kind of team, one that had good defense and ran the ball, in Jacksonville when he returned as head of football operations in 2017. When they played us in the regular season, it was an identity game. *Are we tough enough to compete with the Steelers because they are the standard of toughness?* They did that and then some in a 30–9 win at Heinz Field and they continued that in the divisional round of the playoffs. They made plays offensively and they were patient with the run. I was surprised that quarterback Blake Bortles had the game that he did against us. I really did not think he had that in him.

But we'll go back to the drawing board. One thing that we saw in 2017 was that the New England Patriots are beatable and unfortunately we didn't take advantage of a year when that was the case. The Steelers keep working their way up. We just can't seem to quite reach the top of the hill and hopefully we'll come in with the kind of resolve and keep the focus on football.

Drama came at seemingly every turn of the 2017 season, and some of it was beyond the Steelers' control. The National Anthem controversy engulfed

While clinching the division with a 2017 win against the rival Baltimore Ravens, the hearts of Ben Roethlisberger and the rest of the Steelers were still with Ryan Shazier.

the NFL early in the season. When the Steelers didn't come out for it in Chicago, I understand what they were doing. They basically said, "Look, we don't want to be pawns of this issue. So if we can't agree on it, we're going to stick together." In retrospect, maybe it wasn't the right idea. The players felt bad about it. That's why they apologized for it. But there was a lot of controversy surrounding it, and a lot of people were angry, and I understand why.

I love this country. When my mom and dad became American citizens, I was in sixth grade. My dad had an American flag lapel pin, and my aunt, who had been in the country and was an American citizen, bought us an American flag cake. My parents were so proud, especially my dad. He loved this country and he was so thankful that we came to America. There were a lot of Turkish people in Chicago, and our social life was with other Turkish people. When any Turks complained about America, my dad said, "Well, go back home. This is where you get your bread buttered." My dad wouldn't let any other Turks talk badly about America.

I became an American citizen when I was 21 years old. I remember taking the oath and thinking, *Wow, I'm an American citizen.* I was so proud and I would never not stand for "The Star-Spangled Banner." I love this country, and it means too much to me and the freedom that has been fostered for me, even though I'm not a native-born American.

I have a lot of buddies who are in the military and I understand their outrage. But I thought, *If I ever experienced something like that, how would I feel about the guy kneeling next to me?* The first thing that came to mind was the NFL strike of 1987. Four guys I admired a great deal and loved—John Stallworth, Donnie Shell, Mike Webster, and Gary Dunn—were our captains, and they crossed the picket line. I was so hurt and so disappointed by it. But when the strike ended, I held no animosity toward them and I still loved them, and our friendship was healed. I forgave John, Donnie, Webby, and Gary so how could I not forgive the guy that kneels next to me?

I couldn't help noticing some irony in the whole controversy when we played the Ravens in Baltimore the week after it erupted. There was a group of about eight to 10 fans that came in just for "The Star-Spangled Banner" and then they boycotted the game. They stood right in front of the press box, and I've gotten a little feisty with Ravens fans over the years. They all wore the same T-shirts. The top of the shirt read, "I always stand for the National Anthem," and below it, "I kneel for the cross." I said to one of them, "Hey, I like your T-shirt. Don't you have that backward? Do you really think the American flag should be above the cross of Christ? No way." He said, "Oh, I never thought of that. You're right." They were getting ready to play "The Star-Spangled Banner," and these guys all had beers in their hands. I said, "Hey, why don't you show some respect for the flag! Put your beer on the ground! You shouldn't be drinking beer while 'The Star-Spangled Banner' is being sung. Otherwise, you're just a bunch of hypocrites! Put your beers down and stand at attention as 'The Star-Spangled Banner' is being played!" Billy Hillgrove was busting a gut, laughing at me yelling at Ravens fans.

Mike Tomlin loves the military and is so thankful for it. Throughout this whole process, I met a guy named Ralph at ManUp Pittsburgh, and we really hit it off. He has this ministry called One Love, and it is about unity and everybody coming together. It is based on the 133rd psalm: "How good and pleasant it is when brother live together in unity." In that psalm we see God's pleasure when men live together in unity. Ralph called me and said, "Tunch, I've got a bunch of hats for the Steelers called 'One Love.' Do you think Mike Tomlin would allow us to come and bring these hats?" I asked Mike, and he said, "By all means." In an era where coaches don't want any distractions, Mike welcomed these guys, and the players welcomed them, too.

The thing that far and away hurt us all the most in 2017 was something we couldn't control. It happened when Ryan Shazier went down against the

Cincinnati Bengals with a spinal injury. My heart broke for him, especially after it became clear that he faced a long recovery. I knew from studying film with Ryan how much time he put into getting ready for every game. He worked hard and wanted to be the best. When we were looking at the Steelers Hall of Fame pictures in the practice facility before going to watch film, he said, "I want my picture up on that wall."

Losing Ryan was a major hit on an emotional level and to our talent level. The speed he plays with surprises people. If you're a running back and you've got the ball in the flat on a screen pass or a flare pass, and it looks like you've got all of this green in front of you, all of the sudden here comes Ryan like a missile. It was just like Troy Polamalu. His speed just shocked you.

Ryan was fast and played even faster. He got to the ball in a hurry. That's one aspect the Steelers lost without him, as well as his leadership. He called the defenses and made sure everyone was in position. Also, Vince Williams plays a lot better football when he is next to Ryan because they are great in tandem, playing so well off of each other. Ryan was the more athletic, fast guy, and Vince was more of the thumper. The linebacking play definitely suffered without Ryan.

The position also was a source of drama when the Steelers released James Harrison, and he signed with the Patriots. I don't really fault anybody in that circumstance. James made it clear that he wanted to play and that he wanted to contribute. And I get why the Steelers didn't play him. They wanted to develop younger players. I think everybody did what they had to do.

When you get the thanks for the memories speech and you still want to play, and there's a suitor out there for you, you go play. How many guys get to finish their career with the team they started with? Franco Harris didn't. Webby didn't. When I left for Green Bay, I didn't want to go to the Packers. I wanted to stay here.

When New England signed James, people said, "How could Bill Belichick do that? He wants him just for the playbook." That is the biggest bunch of garbage. I'm sure they did pick his brain, but that's not why they signed him. They picked him up because when they signed James he was already the best outside linebacker on their team. He had two sacks in just the four games he played for them.

Today with social media and the 24-hour news cycle, any perceived drama is blown out of proportion. I don't do social media. I'm not a fan of it. But you can't tell guys to stay off social media. It's like telling them not to call anybody or email anybody when they get home. But I also think these guys have to realize that the less information they give out, the better.

I love what Chuck Noll always said: treat the media like mushrooms. Feed them a bunch of crap and keep them in the dark. That's what I like about Belichick. He's not going to answer anything, and the more you're on social media, the more you divulge, and for every question answered, there is a follow-up question.

During the '87 strike. I would get asked, "Tunch, what do you think about Mike Webster crossing the picket line?" I would say, "Oh, I love Webby. He's my brother. But I'm more concerned with the guys that are still on strike with me." Then it would be, "Does it bother you that he crossed the picket line?" I would say, "I don't agree with it, but I'm more concerned about the guys that are still on strike with me." You don't have to answer the question, and I think guys today feel like they have to stand up for themselves through social media and make points through social media. The more left unsaid, the less distraction you have to deal with.

When there's drama in that locker room, players feel like they have to respond to it. Reporters are going to come up to you and say, "Hey, what do you think about what Le'Veon Bell said?" You have to deal with it when you just want to talk football. I don't know how much it affects you, and some teams love the drama. Maybe the Steelers aren't one of those teams that love the drama. It would be nice to see a season without any of that.

I've been around this league a long time. It's going to be 40 years in 2020, and the one thing I can say without a doubt is that it is all about the relationships. Charlie "Tremendous" Jones, a motivational speaker, came to one of our Bible studies in the early 1980s and he said, "Ten years from now, you'll be the same person you are today with the exception of the people you meet and the books you read." It's true. Patrick Morley, who wrote *The Man in the Mirror* said, "The process is the purpose. Relationships are the goal, and God has the plan." That is also true. Would I love to have a Super Bowl ring? Absolutely. Do I feel that my life is less complete because I didn't win one? Not at all. I still have the deep friendships. I still have the great memories. I still have the great experiences.

CHAPTER 5

Super Bowl Seasons

Hines Ward was probably one of the smartest receivers I've ever seen play the game. He and I did a radio show for 10 years together and he always said that you have to be able to run every route at three different speeds to set up the defensive backs. He made a career doing that and Hines also had unbelievable field awareness. He was always aware of down and distance. Because he played quarterback in college, he thought like a quarterback.

What really endeared him to Steelers fans is how he loved to dish out hits. He laid out Rod Woodson, he laid out Ed Reed, he laid out Bart Scott. When you had a wide receiver like that, you had the defensive players with their head on a swivel because there is nothing as embarrassing as getting laid out by—to paraphrase Chuck Noll—a small number, and Hines wore a small number as a wide receiver. The funny thing about Hines is—as fearless as he was on the football field—he is afraid of just about anything off the football field.

We were on the first Steelers cruise together, and he brought his own life raft in a suitcase. He said, "Hey, I saw *Titanic*. If this thing goes down, I'm going to have my own life raft." I was shocked that he competed in the Ironman Triathlon after he retired because he only wanted to swim in pools and didn't want to venture into open waters. I asked him once, "Do you ever go in the ocean?" He said, "No, man, there's sharks in there. I saw *Jaws*." He also didn't want to go skiing because he saw a movie where these kids got caught on the ski lift and were left up there. He projected these catastrophes onto himself, but he was totally fearless on the field. He wasn't afraid to go

In one of the defining plays of the game, Hines Ward, the MVP of Super Bowl XL, catches a 43-yard touchdown pass from Antwaan Randle El.

over the middle and he wasn't afraid of retaliation. He told me this story where Bart Scott said one time, "I'm gonna kill you." Hines said, "Oh, come on. You really want to kill me?" He said, "Oh yeah, I wanna kill you." Hines said, "I don't want to kill you."

Another seeming quirk about Hines: he told me that he got manicures, and I said, "You got manicures? You're a tough guy." He said, "You've got to take care of your fingernails. I learned that from Charles Johnson. Have you ever noticed how strong my fingers are? That's because I get a manicure every week." This was on the radio so it wasn't like he was trying to keep it quiet. Ward and cornerback Deshea Townsend were such good buddies, and I always said, "Deshea, you've got to be his publicist." He said, "I do! I hear him about to say something and I'm behind the camera, going 'Don't Stop!'" They were a lot of fun.

I always told him, "Hines, you carry the Rodney Dangerfield card further than anybody I've ever met. I get no respect. Everyone says you're a great player, and you keep saying everyone thinks you're too small and you're too slow." He always said he was a low-round draft pick. Third round? I mean, come on! Third round is a high draft pick. I would have given anything to be a third-round draft pick. It's not like he was a sixth or seventh-rounder. It was like he made it up in his mind, and he said, "Oh, nobody thinks I am any good."

It worked for him, and because of that, the Steelers ended their Super Bowl drought in 2005. They capped an incredible postseason run with a win in Detroit, Jerome Bettis' hometown, that sent Jerome into retirement with the ring that had eluded him. Hines won MVP of Super Bowl XL and he was one of the driving forces of the 2005–10 teams that played in three Super Bowls and won two of them.

The missing piece after a handful of near misses through the years was, of course, Ben Roethlisberger. I played with a bunch of different quarterbacks after Terry Bradshaw retired in 1983. A bunch more came through Pittsburgh after I retired before Ben finally gave the Steelers a long-term answer at quarterback.

What impresses me most about Ben is his strength. Guys drill him, and he's still upright. Guys are hanging onto his shoulder, and he throws them off. You've got to wrap him up, pick him up, and put him on the ground. If you just take a shot at him and think he is going down, you're wrong. There are two kinds of quarterbacks who extend plays with their athleticism. The first is a guy with speed and shiftiness. Ben does it with his strength. When you try to sack him, it's like hitting a brick wall. He doesn't just avoid the sacks. He's still looking downfield so after he shrugs a guy off he still knows where he's going with the ball. That's what I think is so impressive about Ben.

You could tell that this guy was going to be a player with the throws he made early in his rookie season in 2004. You could see the arm strength, and he was faster back then. He's also got the intangibles, a sixth sense if you will, for the game. You always talk about the it factor in a guy, and that's what Ben has.

Ben can throw three interceptions early and not lose his confidence and then throw three touchdown passes in the fourth quarter. He doesn't get rattled. You can tell when a quarterback's done by the look in his eyes. A quarterback that's struggling all day comes in the huddle and may have the Brook trout look. He's belly up, he's done. I could tell early in his career that Ben was not fazed by a bad play. He was kind of like Bradshaw, kind of like Brett Favre. *So what if I threw three interceptions? I know I'm going to complete the pass that's going to win the game.* I played with quarterbacks where they walked in the huddle during a bad game and you thought, *We're done.*

The Steelers looked like they were done in 2005 after a midseason slump dropped them to 7–5. That changed in the Chicago Bears game when Jerome turned Brian Urlacher into a hood ornament. That wasn't uncommon for Bussy. He hit you so hard that your children felt it. Early in games guys came up and just tried to unload on him. By the end of the game, guys took convenient angles to miss or they jumped on his back. He sucked the will to fight out of their hearts, and there was nothing to hit. He was just so compact; it was all thighs and shoulders.

Urlacher knows all about that now, and after the Steelers' convincing win in that game against the Bears, I started to think that these guys might have something. I'll be honest that I did not have a lot of confidence going into Cincinnati for the first playoff game. Carson Palmer was playing great football, and the Bengals had a great trio of receivers in Chad Johnson, T.J. Houshmandzadeh, and Chris Henry. Palmer threw that bomb to Henry early, and during the broadcast, you heard me say, "Carson Palmer's down. Forget the play. Carson Palmer is down." We won the game after Palmer left with a knee injury, and the Bengals were pissed, especially since they had beaten us at Heinz Field when Houshmandzadeh used the Terrible Towel as a doormat. Craig Wolfley said at the time, "You better not disrespect the towel. They're in trouble now."

Preparing for the next playoff game against the Indianapolis Colts as an analyst, I watched film of the Colts' game against San Diego because the Chargers played a 3-4 defense and did a lot of the same things that we did. One of the things the Colts did was molly protect their guards. In other words the guard had a dual read. If the inside linebacker didn't blitz, he popped out and picked up the outside linebacker. What you're doing with that strategy is saying we're going to give one of our guys an option, and it's going to take away two of your guys because you can't bring them both. The problem with that is if your outside linebackers are good pass rushers, you're putting your guard in a really hard spot. The Chargers' outside pass rushers weren't as good as our guys, and I said on TV that if the Colts did this, they were going to get killed. An offensive tackle versus an outside linebacker is much better than a guard popping out, and they did not make any adjustments against us. Joey Porter killed them, and then we brought Joey and Troy Polamalu off the same edge at times.

After our fourth-down stop late in the game, I said, "Call the travel agent. We're going to Denver." Two rules of broadcasting are you never step on your play-by-play guy, and you don't turn into a fan. That was one of the times that I lost my mind and turned into a fan.

The thing about it is I saw the disastrous play coming after it looked like the Steelers had sealed the win. I saw the linebacker coming unblocked and saw that Bussy didn't have a great grip on the ball when he got hit. It was almost like I saw it in slow motion as it was happening, especially after Colts cornerback Nick Harper scooped up Bussy's fumble. You heard me saying, "Oh my gosh, somebody tackle him!" I thought he was going all the way, but Ben obviously made a great play to get Harper on the ground. After the fumble I said, "Alright, call that travel agent back. Put those tickets on hold." The fact that Mike Vanderjagt missed the field goal at the end of the game was so great. I was not a fan of his because he was so cocky.

I didn't think the Denver Broncos could beat us in the AFC Championship Game. Out of the three games that the Steelers played on the way to the Super Bowl, I thought Denver would be the easiest game or the least scary opponent. Ben played really well in that game, sending the Steelers to the Super Bowl.

Before Super Bowl XL against the Seattle Seahawks, Bill Hillgrove called Myron Cope from the press box on his cell phone, and Bill put me on the phone. I said, "Hey, Myron, any advice for the Super Bowl?" He said, "Yes, dear Tunch don't say anything stupid." I said, "Alright, Myron, good coaching tip. I'll try not to."

I knew a bunch of the Seahawks coaches because they were all in Green Bay when I was with the Packers for my last NFL season as a player. I knew that the Seahawks were concerned about matching the intensity of the Steelers. If you recall the first couple of offensive series for the Seahawks, they went sideline to sideline: bubble screens, quick outs, flare passes. They wanted to slow down Joey and Clark Haggans. They wanted to slow down Aaron Smith and Kimo von Oelhoffen. They tried to make the Steelers play as flat-footed as possible and tire them out. They had a really nice gameplan early.

That year the Steelers ran a number of gadget plays—like reverses and reverse passes—that they kept building on, and it culminated with Antwaan Randle El's throw to Hines for the game-winning touchdown. There were two points in that game where I thought *game over*: Willie Parker's 75-yard run, which is still a Super Bowl record, and that play. Both resulted from the mentality of: we're going to pound the ball, pound the ball, pound the ball and we don't think you can stop us. Chuck always said, "I don't care if everyone in the stadium knows what you're doing. If everyone makes their block, they're not going to stop it." He was right, and if teams start over-loading to stop the run, the gadget plays are going to work for you. That playoff run was a lot of fun. It was the Bussey tour and the story of him going back home, and the players paid homage to Dick LeBeau by wearing his Lions jersey when they went to Detroit. That team had the chemistry, that closeness, and it was really cool to watch.

The 2008 Steelers also really enjoyed playing together. They had a confidence about them and they had all of the components of a champion. It turned out to be a phenomenal year and ended with the Steelers winning a record sixth Lombardi Trophy.

If you get 20 sacks from your two outside linebackers in a 3-4 defense, you are well on your way to having a dominant pass rushing team. LaMarr

Woodley and James Harrison had 27.5 sacks between them in 2008. Then if you get 10 sacks from your inside linebackers, which the Steelers did, teams have to pick their poison when they are preparing for you. When the Steelers blitz, do you keep the tight end in to block, or does your running back have to stay in to pick up the blitzer? And then the question is: do you slide the protection to the outside linebacker, or do you keep it base protection where you focus on the inside? Whichever you decide, Dick LeBeau is usually one move ahead of you.

With a nose tackle like Casey Hampton and two-gap defensive ends like Aaron and Brett Keisel, it basically prevented opponents from running on us. Those guys were that good, and with LaMarr and James setting the edge, you couldn't get outside on that defense. There wasn't a tight end who could block either one of those guys. You couldn't get on the edge or in between the tackles. So you had to throw the ball and you had to get rid of it fast because you were going to get the zone blitzes with the two inside linebackers coming and an outside linebacker dropping off.

It was funny because the Friday night before the Super Bowl, Wolf and I were watching film. The Steelers had already had their last practice, and linebackers coach Keith Butler was beside himself about James Farrior. I said, "Buttsy, are you all right?" He said, "Are you kidding me? Farrior had three mental mistakes today; he never has three mental mistakes, oh my gosh." He was kind of freaking out, and Wolf and I were laughing.

He probably calmed down a little when James made one of the greatest plays in Super Bowl history. Arizona Cardinals quarterback Kurt Warner came up to the line of scrimmage and saw Woodley and Harrison on the outside. He thought James was coming, but James was already back in coverage. Warner went to his hot read, which was in the flat, but guess who was already in the flat? That was a great LeBeau call. That Steelers was a great defense, making a great play at the right time. When the guys transitioned into offensive mode, it was like an NBA team on a fast break. They were gone, and Harrison scored on a 100-yard interception return on the final play of the first half.

In Friday's practice before the Super Bowl, Mike Tomlin really focused on transition. *Hey, if you get the ball, start running. Think score, think score.* If you watch the replay of Harrison's interception return for a touchdown, the first thing you see is Deshea Townsend asking for the ball. Even though he didn't get the ball, Deshea got out in front, and everybody else was blocking, too. It was a great coaching tip that guys assimilated and put it into application.

I sat next to James Farrior on the bus that took us back from the Super Bowl parade, and he said, "This Super Bowl feels a little different." I said, "Could it be because it's your defense now?" He thought about it and said, "You're right."

From a personality standpoint, Potsie—that is what everybody called Farrior—was not the gruff, Lambert type, but he was just a great player. He was a tough guy, who could run and tackle. He played hurt. And I think he was one of the smartest guys out there, if not the smartest, because he called the defense. Mike Tomlin said there were a lot of alpha males on that defense and in that locker room, but Potsie was the leader.

I read in Bill Belichick's book, *Patriot Games*, that Tom Brady could take a vicious shot, come back to the huddle, call the next play, and be fine. Belichick said that's the kind of toughness he wanted in his quarterback. Well, that's the kind of toughness you had in Farrior. When you call the defenses, know everything that's going on, and are the smartest guy in the room outside of the coaches, guys respect you. Factor in that you're a tough guy, that you work as hard as anybody else, and all of the sudden, you are the alpha male.

Harrison was also a dominant personality and just a tremendous, tremendous player. In 2008 he played lights out. He was just such a unique player for the Steelers. Chuck always talked about hitting with a rising blow, meaning that you get your legs under you and pop a guy. James epitomized that. In his prime he was so explosive and had such an incredible work ethic. He is so strong, but there is weight room strength and playing strength, and he had both.

The fact that he got cut four times—and this is coming from someone who was cut—he had this desire and really had a chip on his shoulder. It drove him to be the most physical, the nastiest, the hardest worker. In today's NFL offensive tackles are all around 6'5", 6'6". Well, he was a 6'0" guy who weighed 255 pounds, benched 500 pounds, and deadlifted 600 and he was going to run over the 6'6" guy. That's what made James so good, and at the point of attack, there was not a tight end or running back in the world who was going to be able to block him.

I can't compare him to anybody because his body type is different. I've never seen a body type like that at outside linebacker. They're usually longer, leaner, and more athletic. He's compact, short, squatty. He has arms like legs and legs like people. He did a great job of playing the edge and he had just enough speed to get by you. He wasn't going to scare you with his speed, but if the pass set was too heavy on him, he gave you a finesse move. If you set too light on him, forget about it. You were getting picked up and thrown in the quarterback's lap, which for an offensive tackle is probably the most embarrassing thing that could ever happen.

Troy was another player from those defenses who was so unique. He had that sixth sense, whether it was jumping over the top or baiting you into making a throw. He did a great job of playing angles. On his sack/forced fumble against Baltimore Ravens quarterback Joe Flacco in 2010, the Steelers had run that blitz earlier in the game, and Troy was a step slow in getting to Flacco. When they ran it again, James did a great job of pulling the tight end down and giving Troy the shorter edge. Troy knew the edge was going to be cut short and he adjusted and made the game-turning play.

Wolf called him "the flyin' Hawaiian human crash test dummy," and that was a great description because Troy played with abandon and without regard for his own body. You saw the Superman plays where he would dive over the top. He was a great blitzer and he was great in run support. He was good in man-to-man coverage and great in zone coverage. When the ball was in the air, he found it, and when he got the ball, he was thinking touchdown. Polamalu made so many big plays during his prime from 2005 to 2010.

The defensive line didn't get a lot of glory on those teams, but it was a huge reason—literally and figuratively—why the Steelers were so successful. Aaron and Brett, former basketball players, had great feet and did a great job of staying square to the line of scrimmage. They played the gaps and they did not get taken off the ball. Aaron reminded me of Howie Long. He played the run and the pass well. He was not quite the player Long was, but you weren't going to move him at the point of attack. What made him so good, too, was his play on the backside. He had a great feel for playing his gap and not overrunning the plays and getting out of position. And yet he made a ton of plays. He was such a tough guy. Wolf always said that Smith reminded him of John Wayne and Mike Webster because he was just that lunch bucket type.

Casey was the immovable object at nose tackle. He was strong as a bull and he played with great leverage. He was just lower than everybody else. You're not going to dig a 350-pound nose tackle out if you can't get under him, and Casey was also great with his hands. He always controlled the center and he did a great job of not getting moved.

Casey was just a fun-loving guy and he was one of those guys who knew how to turn it on and off. When he was getting ready to play, he was all business. But in the locker room, he was a cut up. I went up to Casey in training camp and said, "How much do you weigh?" He looked at me and said, "How much do you think I weigh?" I said, "350?" He said, "*350?*" He looked like he was hurt. He walked away, looked over his shoulder, and said, "I'm the best-looking 350 you ever saw."

I would be remiss if I didn't talk about Heath Miller and his value to those teams. I played with some good tight ends, but Heath was the best I saw for the Steelers during both my time as a player and a broadcaster. He was just such a pro. He took just as much pride in blocking as he did in catching the ball. Then there was his toughness. One game against the Bengals, either Reggie Nelson or George Iloka gave him a cheap shot. The next time Heath caught the ball, he was running down the sideline, made a beeline back to the middle of the field, lowered his shoulder, and just lit him up. That was the way he played. He had that physicality, that toughness, and he was smart. I don't think he ever said anything about himself. The fans yelled "Heeeath!" But he was almost like, "Aw, shucks." He had great hands, too. There are not a lot of NFL tight ends who I would call a complete tight end; I think he might have been one of the last of a dying breed.

That core group made it back to the Super Bowl in 2010, and that season showed why Mike is a great coach. Ben missed the first four games of the season, and there were other offseason distractions that could have torpedoed the season before it started. But Mike does not let excuses ever enter players' minds and he didn't that year. Regarding guys holding out, Chuck always said: "We're going to coach who's here." Everyone took it as a slight against Franco Harris when the running back held out, but Chuck was just emphasizing that he was not going to let those guys become distractions. Mike is like that, too.

In one of the most memorable NFL plays of all time, James Harrison returns an interception 100 yards for a touchdown just before halftime of Super Bowl XLIII.

Offensive coordinator Bruce Arians did a great job of coaching the quarterbacks while Ben was out and keeping it simple for them. I remember saying, "If we go 2–2, we'll be great." We went 3–1, and because of that, I think that team believed it was invincible. I think that's what got them to the Super Bowl. I still marvel at the job that coaching staff did.

I thought the Steelers were going to beat the Packers in Super Bowl XLV. I thought they were a much more physical football team and I thought the physicality of the Steelers was going to win the day, but it didn't. I was shocked they lost that game, but Aaron Rodgers is a magician.

Brady is the best quarterback I've ever seen, but Rodgers does things I've never seen before. When a quarterback ducks a sack, he has to reset his feet and throw. Well, Rodgers ducks a sack and he comes up throwing without setting his feet. He's got that knack—kind of like a third baseman fielding a bunt who comes up throwing—and it comes out of there like a frozen rope. That game we lost not to the Packers; we lost to Rodgers.

That season a little-known Steelers rookie showed flashes, and since then Antonio Brown has become a superstar. You could tell he was going to be special early in his career. I said at one point: "Whoa, this guy's fast. He's quick. He's a jitterbug who can dodge rain drops, and the main thing is he's going to battle for the ball." His work ethic sets him apart, too.

I've watched videos of his training regimen, and they're insane. I've never seen him loaf. I once heard a great quote from Gordie Howe about Wayne Gretzky. He said that every time Gretzky took the ice he took it as if nobody had seen him play. That's how I feel about Antonio. Every time Antonio takes the field—whether it's in practice, minicamp, or OTAs—it's as if nobody has seen him play. Every play, his competitive nature is at 100 rpm. He wants to win every throw, every route, every jump ball.

Every time he catches the ball during team drills, he outruns everyone to the end zone. Franco used to do that, too. I asked him once, "Franco, every time?" He said, "Yeah, I want to get used to scoring touchdowns." Antonio makes sure that he outruns every guy who is in pursuit during a drill. He takes it as a challenge, a competition, and I think that's what makes him so great. He'll stay after practice and work with the JUGS machine. He works on catching passes one-handed, he works on catching punts. The guy is constantly working to be the best. I'm sure there are guys that compete as hard as him at the wide receiver position, but I don't know who they are.

CHAPTER 6

Long and Winding Road to Pittsburgh

I had two uncle Alis, and the one who was my dad's cousin was hysterical. He had that big, kind of Ottoman Empire mustache and he was a tough guy. He always wanted to wrestle me, even though he was only 5'7". One time when he was staying with us, we were getting ready to go out to dinner. Uncle Ali looked really nice and said in this really thick accent, "What do you think of my outfit? It is a good composition, no?" I said, "Composition? Yeah, you look great Uncle Ali." He said, "I speak good English, no?" I said, "No."

He embraced me—Turkish men hug like they are tying up a wrestler—and said, "Do you want to wrestle?" I was probably a junior in high school at the time and I was big. I said, "Uncle Ali, I'm not going to wrestle you." He said, "C'mon, wrestle. *Gourash* [Turkish for wrestle]. C'mon, we wrestle, we wrestle, we wrestle."

He tried to take me down, so I crossfaced him and put him on his back. My whole life he had been wrestling me and squeezing my cheeks and just having fun with me. But he couldn't take me anymore, and twice in a row, I put him on his back. After the second time, he reached up, grabbed me by the family jewels, and twisted. All of the sudden, he reversed me and was on top and he had his knee in my chest. He said, "You are a football player. You think you are tough. You are nothing when I have got you by the balls."

That is a snapshot of the culture I grew up in.

Turks are very confrontational. My family would wrestle, fight, and argue. My dad, Mehmet, and I even fenced in the house. My dad loved to fence, and we had these plastic swords. We were on the third floor of an apartment building and when we fenced the whole building shook. That inevitably led to calls from the neighbors.

There was always a little bit of emotional shrapnel in our house. I just thought it was normal. My parents would argue, and my dad would say,

Long before the Pittsburgh Steelers drafted me, I had a winding road to the NFL. (Pittsburgh Steelers)

"You're going to give me a heart attack!" And my mom would say, "You're going to give me a stroke!" The first time I brought Sharon, my future wife, home from college, my parents got into a big argument. She looked at me and said, "Is everything all right?" I said, "Oh yeah, it's normal, just dinner conversation."

My mom, Ayten, did not want to come to America and she was kind of hoping after a couple of years that we would go back. My dad had a relentless work ethic and he was hard-nosed and as stubborn as the day is long. No way were we going back to Turkey. It worked well in his desire to live the American Dream; it wasn't so great for relations. I saw what that hard-headedness did from a relationship standpoint and I didn't want that. But I saw what the hard-headedness would do from a work standpoint and I wanted that.

I've heard psychologists say that you are born with a particular bent—mentally and physically—and then you're influenced by your parents and your surroundings. Then you kind of pick and choose what works for you. My mom was much more nurturing so I probably get that from her.

My parents were so different. My dad once had a massive heart attack and he just passed it off as gas. This happened when they were moving from the suburbs of Chicago to San Francisco. After a while he got off the train because he knew what was happening. As the paramedics were coming for him, he said, "Wait a minute, I have to call my boss and tell him I'm not coming into work." My mom's probably the opposite. She worries about everything; every illness could be terrible.

My dad made a tremendous sacrifice to come to America. He left a very lucrative position with a company that he started in textiles. He went from living in a very nice house with full-time health benefits to living in a one-bedroom apartment in Chicago in the uptown section. My parents slept on a Murphy bed—it's a bed that comes out of the closet—and I slept on a cot in the kitchen. My mom said, "So this is America?"

My parents met in Istanbul where my mother was born. I was born there too, in 1957, two years after my parents got married. My dad wanted to follow my Uncle Ali, who was his brother, to America. Uncle Ali was a surgeon in the Chicago area, and my parents also had some Turkish friends living in the area. The attitude was: come to America, the land of opportunity.

We came to the United States when I was two years old. My dad started working for an investments firm in Chicago. He was an accountant by trade, just a real mathematical mind. He worked Saturdays and sometimes Sundays. We lived in four different neighborhoods in the inner city of Chicago and just kind of moved around until junior high school.

We moved to the suburbs, about 30 miles north of Chicago, after a guy tried to force himself into our apartment when my mom was home by herself. I think it was 1969 when we finally bought our first house in Highland Park and I remember how excited my parents were. Shortly after that my parents became American citizens. My mother thought it would be better to wait until I turned 21 before I became an American citizen, so it would be easier for me to go back and forth to Turkey.

In her mind she always thought I would go back to Turkey and find a Turkish bride. The reality is I never went back to Turkey—except when I was seven—because once sports started, I was always doing that in the summer.

Growing up in Chicago, we didn't have the youth sports they had in the suburbs. In my neighborhood I played pick-up baseball, pick-up football, and pick-up street hockey. I learned how to play ice hockey at my aunt's house. Aunt Ayten lived out in the suburbs and she taught me how to skate. She wasn't my real aunt, but she was my mom's best friend and she bought me my first hockey stick. We spent a lot of time at her place, and she lived on a small lake that would freeze over in the winter.

I always loved football more than anything. We moved to the suburbs when I was in sixth grade, and I played organized flag football for the first time and in seventh grade I played organized football. In high school I played baseball until my junior year and then I switched to track so I could lift weights. I never played in a hockey league because it was too expensive, and we couldn't afford it. But I played rec hockey and pick-up hockey all the time. I didn't play football my freshman year because I had a real bad case of Osgood-Schlatter disease, which is a knee condition frequently caused by growth spurts, but that was only a temporary setback.

I loved baseball and had a decent bat was not a great fielder. I caught some, but my arm was terrible. My sophomore year I threw out about two of 20 guys who stole on me that year, but hitting the ball came easy to me. I did track and field for the workout and so I could lift weights after school. I would get my throws in as a shot putter and I was a high jumper as well. (I wasn't exactly Dick Fosbury.) I'd finish practice by running with the sprinters, so I could set myself in the best shape possible for football.

Football came the most naturally to me, though my mom did not want me to play. She thought the sport was too rough. My dad liked it and he came to the games, but my mother never joined him. It was too hard for her to watch. Eastern Illinois and Indiana State were the only schools that offered me scholarships. I went to Indiana State because nobody from my high school was going there. I thought it would be kind of cool to go to a place where I didn't know anybody.

My future wife achieved fame before I did when she and another Indiana State cheerleader appeared with Larry Bird on the cover of *Sports Illustrated*. It was for the 1977 college basketball preview edition, and the cover featured Larry with the caption, "COLLEGE BASKETBALL'S SECRET

WEAPON." It was crazy because Sharon, who is to the left of Larry on the cover, and I had just started dating.

I had met her as a freshman as we were in the same dorm and ate at the same time. I remember saying, "Who is that?" One of the guys on my team said, "That's Sharon Senefeld." I said, "Man, she is cute." He said, "She's as nice as she is cute." She was really good friends with my roommates, and I actually dated two of her roommates before I dated her.

I had always wanted to date her, but I was too chicken to ask her because she was a cheerleader and everybody loved her. The scouting report on her was she only dated as friends because she had a boyfriend back home. I didn't ask her out until my junior year, and that's when we started dating. After she was on the cover of *Sports Illustrated*, she started getting all of these letters from guys. *Will you marry me? Can I take you to the Sugar Bowl?* It was the weirdest thing, but she never let it get to her head. She would say about the *SI* cover, "I don't even know why they asked me." She just played it off. My kids joked, "Mom was on the cover of *Sports Illustrated*, but Dad never made the magazine." I did make the magazine though for the worst game of my NFL career. It was against Lyle Alzado and the Los Angeles Raiders in the 1983 playoffs. There is a picture of Alzado sacking Cliff Stoudt, and I'm on the ground after he had already run over me.

Larry was a year older than I and he had first gone to Indiana University. He didn't like it and went back to French Lick where he became a garbage-man. His buddy, Danny King, was the point guard at Indiana State and he said to Larry, "Why don't you come walk on here? I'm sure you'll get a scholarship and you'll like it. It's a smaller school." Larry came and practiced with the team my freshman year, but he wasn't eligible to play.

Two of his high school buddies were on my floor and they would talk about how great of a high school basketball player he was. My freshman year I got hurt in preseason camp and I didn't travel or suit up for any games that season. One weekend when the team was on the road I went home with those guys to French Lick for the Pumpkin Festival. That's when I really heard about the legend of Larry Bird. That offseason I lifted in the physical education building where the basketball team practiced. I would just go watch practice and say, "Man, that's too bad that guy can't play. I'll bet he's going to be pretty good."

It was a great time to be at Indiana State. In addition to Larry Bird, we had gymnast Kurt Thomas, who would have been in the 1980 Olympics had the Americans not boycotted the games to protest the Soviet Union's invasion of Afghanistan. We also had Bruce Baumgartner, who has four Olympic medals—two golds, a silver, and a bronze—in wrestling. Bruce is now the athletic director at Edinboro University of Pennsylvania. His wife, Linda, was a trainer for the football team, and I always used to go to her to tape my ankles because she was the only one who wouldn't cut the circulation off.

We had three world-class athletes in Larry, Kurt, and Bruce. Then there was Wallace Johnson, who played for the Montreal Expos and the San Francisco Giants. Zane Smith, who later pitched for the Pirates, was also from Indiana State. I didn't know Zane, but I knew Wallace really well. When he was with the Expos, Johnson came into town to play the Pittsburgh Pirates, and I connected with him because everything we did was at Three Rivers Stadium. We ran there and lifted there so you'd get to know the Pirates and the Pirates' opponents. I got to meet Pete Rose and Tommy Lasorda. I once asked Dirt DiNardo, the head groundskeeper at Three Rivers Stadium, if he could get me an autograph from Pete Rose. Dirt walked me over to him and said, "Pete, this is Tunch Ilkin, our starting right tackle. He wants your autograph."

This was when Pete was managing the Cincinnati Reds, and I sat down next to him, and we just started shooting the breeze like we were old buddies. Johnny Bench, who was doing Reds games on radio, walked by, and Rose said, "Hey Johnny, autograph this ball for Tunch." He autographed it, and Tony Perez walked by, and Rose got him to autograph it. Rose was the nicest guy, and I was a big Pete Rose fan, the whole "Charlie Hustle" thing.

One of my biggest regrets was when Tommy Lasorda pitched batting practice as strength coach Jon Kolb, Craig Wolfley, and I watched. Kolby said, "It doesn't look that fast," and Lasorda said, "Come on in and take your cuts." I chickened out. We were all just so exhausted as Kolby had just put us through one of his grueling conditioning workouts, like 40 40-yard sprints. I just wanted to go in and take a shower. To this day I second-guess my decision. *I could have taken batting practice with Tommy Lasorda!*

I have another great story when it comes to baseball. One time when Sharon and I were in New York City, we walked into Mickey Mantle's restaurant, and Mantle was sitting at a table. It was one of those wintry days, and we went there for lunch. The foyer was wet, and Sharon had a hold of my arm. I let go of the arm and said, "It's the Mick!" She fell backward before she finally steadied herself. She grabbed my arm and said, "I almost fell down! Why didn't you catch me?" I said, "The Mick. It's the Mick!" We were sitting at our table, and I said, "Sharon, go get Mickey Mantle's autograph. Get it for [our son] Tanner." She said, "I'm not getting it for Tanner. Tanner doesn't know who Mickey Mantle is! You go ask him." I chickened out. I still can't believe I choked like that, but I was starstruck.

I received a chilling and heartbreaking reminder of the cost football can exact early in my college career when my roommate, Fred Rensing, broke his neck in practice and became a quadriplegic. He was one of my best friends, and I was right next to him when it happened.

We were running a punt drill, and he tackled the punt returner. I didn't see it, but I heard the hit. He ducked his head and partially severed his spinal cord and dislocated his fourth and fifth vertebrae. They kept him alive on a ventilator the first two days. I went to the hospital and when I was outside of the emergency room I saw a priest walk in to give him his last rites. He survived, and we remained close until the day he went to be with the Lord.

I visited him in Belleville, Illinois, and sometimes I went by myself and sometimes I took the entire family. Sometimes I just went with Tanner because Tanner and Fred had a really close relationship. My sweet son—he was probably 11—heard Sharon and I talking about how Uncle Fred might need a new kidney, and Tanner said matter of factly, "He can have one of mine." Fortunately, Fred did not end up needing a new kidney, but that shows the special relationship Tanner had with Fred. He called him "Uncle Fred," and many of the times that I went to visit Fred I took Tanner with me.

Fred never had any regrets about playing football. He always said he would do nothing different. As a matter of fact, he said, "I can't wait to get to heaven because I want to play football up there." He always loved the game. The injury to Fred didn't affect me one iota as strange as that sounds. You just don't think it will ever happen to you, and most football players are wired that way.

But any time someone has a spinal cord injury in the NFL—from Mike Utley to Dennis Byrd—my mind goes to Fred and the day when I saw him lying there. It was just so scary and I relive that every time I see a spinal cord injury. That happened in 2017 when Steelers linebacker Ryan Shazier went down in a game at Cincinnati. Initially I thought he would be okay. Everyone initially compared it to the Tommy Maddox injury against the Tennessee Titans when he suffered a spinal concussion but made a full recovery. I thought the same and just kind of got lulled into that. *Okay, it's just like Tommy Maddox. He's going to be walking in a couple of days.* I was not prepared for the severity of that injury, which left Ryan unable to walk in the months that followed.

My career at Indiana State didn't exactly get off to an auspicious start. I thought I was going to play defensive end/outside linebacker and the first day of practice I was the fifth or sixth-team center. I had lifted in high school, but I had never lifted real weights. We had machines in my high school—not free weights. The first time I did a bench press at Indiana State I thought to myself, "Well, I can do 225 pounds on a machine." I tried that weight, and the bar flipped up, and the plates fell off on the other side. It happened in front of a bunch of teammates and it was so embarrassing.

That year I almost felt like those guys were too good for me. I was only 215 to 220 pounds when I went to Indiana State, and the other freshmen offensive linemen were so much bigger than I was. The nose tackles were big, too, and I got my butt kicked on a regular basis. Then I sprained the medial collateral ligament in my knee and I missed the rest of the season.

One positive that came out of that was I got serious about lifting and really learned how. I went from way down on the depth chart center to backup center early in spring ball of my freshman year. It was almost like I had figured it out. I was a backup to Ron Carpenter, and he was a great guy and he was really good about mentoring.

My offensive line coach was Bill Dole, and he and I were really close. I got into fights all of the time, and he loved that I was feisty. Every place I went, it took me a while to feel like I belonged. I always felt I had to earn my way, and sometimes that was through fighting. If a guy gave me an extra push, I went after him. One time I got in a fight with a nose tackle and I went off. The nose tackle was David Lowe, and he and I ended up being roommates and great buddies. But he was a year older than me and took the veteran I'm-going-to-put-you-in-your-place approach one play. It was hot, and I went off. Coach Dole came over with a cup of water. He flicked water at me and said, "Cool down now, buddy, cool down" while he laughed.

He was a great guy and he was one of the first guys who told me I could play in the NFL if I kept working. When he passed away, he was buried in Arlington Cemetery since he had been a captain during the Vietnam War.

That staff got fired midway through my college career, and I had two years with the new staff headed by Dick Jamieson, who later bounced around the NFL a little bit and had been the offensive coordinator at Missouri.

My offensive line coach after Bill was Pete Hoener. He had also been with the Chicago Bears and Arizona Cardinals. He is currently the tight ends coach for the Carolina Panthers and he had previously been with the San Francisco 49ers. I didn't realize it at the time, but he was just a few years older than I was. He was another great guy and a great coach, and I had the same mentality as I had when Bill coached the offensive line. I was still the fighter. I was still the scrapper. Even when I belonged, I felt like I needed to belong.

Dave McGinnis was our defensive backs coach and another one from that staff who later coached in the NFL. Dave, in fact, rose steadily through the ranks and was the head coach of the Arizona Cardinals from 2000 to 2003. He was another coach who told me I had what it took to play in the NFL, and my senior season scouts started coming out. I said, "Are they really here to see me?"

The Steelers were the only team that visited me twice before the 1980 NFL Draft, and it is a wonder I didn't chase them away. On the Steelers' second visit, I snapped the ball to Rollie Dotsch, the Steelers' offensive line coach, I gashed him with my thumbnail, and he bled like crazy. I also was long snapping to scout Bill Nunn and I skipped the ball. When he bent over, he split his pants. I thought, *That's the last I'm going to hear from the Steelers.*

I heard from them anyway, and their phone call sent my mom into a panic. The day of the draft, the Steelers were unable to reach me because I was not expecting to get drafted. I was told I would get drafted in the late rounds, possibly be a free agent, so I was not waiting by the phone when the Steelers drafted me at the end of the first day.

I was at Indiana State, and the Steelers called my parents' home, and my mom answered the phone. She didn't speak good English, and I hadn't told her to be prepared. Chuck Noll said, "Congratulations, Mrs. Ilkin. We just drafted your son Tunch in the sixth round." She thought I was drafted into the Army and freaked out. My mother called me and couldn't get a hold of me. So she called Sharon, who called me and said, "Congratulations, you got drafted by the Steelers in the sixth round."

I said, "Shut up." She said, "Your mom just called me. She thought you got drafted into the Army." I said, "Someone's playing a trick. They didn't draft me." She said, "No, they did!" I said, "How do you know?" She said, "Well, I don't, but who would do that to you?" I said, "A lot of people would." I had call waiting, and a call came in, and I told Sharon, "Let me call you back." I clicked over, and it was Chuck. I talked to him and then Rollie, who said, "Work on your long snapping, Tunch. That's the only way you can make this team—as a long snapper. We need someone, so Webby doesn't have to run down on punts."

Welcome to the Steelers, indeed.

CHAPTER 7

Rookie Blues

My rookie year we played on Monday night the last game of the season, and we were halfway across the country when we got eliminated from playoff contention. We were 9–6, but we didn't get the help we needed before we arrived in San Diego for a game against the Chargers. That night Craig Wolfley and I went to dinner and sat in the outdoor part of the restaurant in the Marriott at Mission Bay. It was beautiful, right on the bay. We were eating dinner when I saw this really tall, lanky, blond-haired guy in a three-piece suit roller skating down the boardwalk toward the hotel. He kind of looked like Ichabod Crane. Wolf and I were looking at him, and it was Jack Lambert. We just started cracking up.

The next night Wolf and I got on the elevator on our way to the game, and there was Howard Cosell, who was obviously going to the game, too, and there was a young lady in the elevator with us. Cosell had this trench coat draped over his shoulders, and it wasn't buttoned. We smiled and we nodded at him. He didn't say anything at first. He looked at us and looked at the young lady and in that Cosell baritone said, "Mon-day night mad-ness." That was all that he said. Wolf and I looked at each other like,

"Yeah!" It was the craziest thing, but it was so Cosell. We didn't even introduce ourselves, and if I had to do it over again, I would have said, "Hi, I'm Tunch Ilkin" because my buddies always told me that Don Meredith, one of Cosell's broadcast partners for *Monday Night Football*, really liked saying my name.

Those encounters may have been a fitting end to what was a crazy and at times surreal first season for me in the NFL. Consider that I spent part of the season playing in a touch football league in suburban Chicago. I got hurt in training camp after someone fell on my leg, and that really set me back. It was the day before the veterans reported to camp, and I didn't practice for the next two-and-a-half weeks because of a knee sprain. I only got in one preseason game—against the New York Jets—and for all of three plays. I had a mental error, a holding penalty that got quarterback Cliff Stoudt hit, and I got yanked. I was cut that Monday.

The Steelers put Billy Hurley, Bobby Kohrs, and John Goodman— they were rookies just like me—on injured reserve before the start of the season. Back then teams used to hide guys there and say they were hurt. Camp had already broken, and we were at Three Rivers Stadium when Ralph Berlin, the trainer, said, "Hey, Chuck Noll wants to see you in his office." I thought, *Uh oh.* But then I thought, *Wait a second, he didn't say, "Bring your playbook." Everybody knows when they cut you they say, "Bring your playbook."*

A lot of the older guys like Ted Petersen and Steve Courson were buddies of mine, and they said, "They'll probably put you on IR. They're going to want to keep you for the future." I walked down the hall, nervous as all get out. I got to Chuck's office, and he stood up. He reached out and shook my hand and said, "Tunch, we had to ask waivers on you this morning." *Waivers? What does that mean?* I figured it couldn't be all that bad if he had to ask permission.

Though I have my gameface on, my first year with the Steelers had its share of ups and downs. (Pittsburgh Steelers)

Then it dawned on me that he was cutting me. I thought to myself, *Oh my. It's over.* He said, "Tunch, now we want you to stay in shape because if someone gets hurt we're going to call you back." I thought he just said that so I wouldn't cry. I cried anyway. I walked into the locker room to say my good-byes, which was really hard. *Caddyshack* had recently come out, and I walked in and quoted Bill Murray to Wolf. "In the immortal words of Jean-Paul Sartre, au revoir, gopher."

I left, thinking to myself, *Where am I going to go? What am I going to do?* My parents had moved to San Francisco. Sharon was teaching school in Richmond, Indiana. I didn't want to go back to Indiana State with my tail between my legs. I went back to Chicago and I called my dad and said, "What do I do?" He said, "Get a job. You've got your degree."

I could have started working for a furniture company or a marketing company. A buddy of mine's dad was in the furniture business and he said, "Tunch, I can get you a job as a furniture rep. You'd make good money." But as soon as I reviewed the hours, I knew that there was no way I would have time to work out. I got a job at a Chicago health club so I was lifting every day, running on my lunch hour, staying in shape. I lived on my buddy Marty's back porch. It was nice weather, and I gave him a couple of bucks for rent.

Jack Worth was my first agent and he had been calling around trying to get me somewhere else. He said, "The worst-case scenario you'll be in camp next year." I thought maybe Canada would call or someone else. In the meantime I was playing in the Highland Park Touch Football League, where I think I was leading the league in sacks. I was using everything I learned in camp. One night in the middle of October, we were at this bar called the Wooden Nickel. We had just finished playing a game, and the New York Giants and Washington Redskins were on TV. Both of those offensive lines were terrible. I said, "I'm at least as good as one of these guys." Someone said, "No, you're with us."

I got a call at 5:00 or 6:00 AM, and it was Chuck. He said, "Are you in shape?" I said, "Yes sir." He said, "Steve Courson broke his foot. We need you. Can you get on the next flight? It's at 9:30." I said, "Absolutely."

I didn't have a stitch of clean clothing. I was wearing a Chicago Health Club sweatsuit and I had a duffel bag of dirty laundry. I went from playing touch football Monday nights to playing the next Monday night at Three Rivers Stadium against the Oakland Raiders. I was on every special teams and I was looking around saying, "Last week I'm playing touch football. This week I'm playing for the Steelers. Is this a great country or what?" Two of my buddies from the touch football team drove my truck out to Pittsburgh to that Monday night game.

I signed with the Steelers, understanding that every contract was week to week, but I was just excited to be back. The first person I saw when I returned was Wolf. I said, "Wolf, I'm back." He said, "You are? That's awesome!" The first couple of nights back, while I was looking for a place, I stayed with him.

Everybody was living in the South Hills of Pittsburgh back then. The night before games we stayed in the Sheraton in Bethel Park right across the street from South Hills Village because Chuck lived right down the street from there in Upper St. Clair. There was a lady who worked at the hotel desk, and I said, "You wouldn't know of any furnished apartments around here?" She said, "I do as a matter of fact. My friend lives in Surrey Garden Apartments in Bethel Park. They're furnished." I got a basement apartment right by the McDonald's in Bethel Park and I finished the season there.

It was awe-inspiring to be in that locker room as a rookie, especially before I got cut.

I remember thinking to myself—or I may have even said something to Wolf—would it be inappropriate if I asked for an autograph? I was joking, but I thought if I got cut, I didn't want to go home empty handed.

Playing in the NFL was sometimes intimidating. I remember the first time I went against linebacker Dirt Winston. I had a ton of respect for him, and he was nasty. We got into a fight, so there was this part of you that was intimidated...until you lined up. Then all of the sudden, you flipped, and it was more, *Oh man, I've got to show that I belong.*

These guys were household names, and many of them future Hall of Famers, and I was practicing against them. When I practiced against Joe Greene, I was thinking, *I just blocked Joe Greene!* It was the craziest thing. Not that I could block Joe without holding him. One time he said, "Don't hold me, rook." I walked back to the huddle saying to myself, 'How am I going to block him if I don't hold him?' I held him the next play, and he punched me right in the belly button. It felt like my belly button hit my spine.

I walked back to the huddle and said, "Quick tip, Wolf: don't hold Joe Greene." He kicked my butt every day in practice. One day Joe said, "Tunch, when you're pass blocking, don't leave your hands out there. Pop, recoil, and pop again." I did that and all of the sudden I started blocking him. Toward the end of the season, we were walking off the field, and Joe said, "You're getting better, Tunch." I couldn't wait to get home and call my dad and tell him, "Joe Greene said I'm getting better, Dad!"

I only made $25,000 my rookie year and like a dummy I spent it all. I didn't have enough money to live in Pittsburgh in the offseason. Not that $25,000 went a long way, but I thought to myself, *What am I going to do?* Wolf had gone back to Buffalo to train with Don Reinhoudt, who won the world's strongest man competition in 1979. I thought the only way I could get by and live here is if I played for the Steelers basketball team because they made some nice money playing in those charity games. You made $100 a night and you played four nights a week. That was almost more money than I was making per day playing for the Steelers.

I said to Joe Gordon, the longtime head of the media relations department, "I want to stay here in the offseason. I want to train here, but I can't afford it. I'm out of money. Can I play for the Steelers basketball team?" He said, "I'm not in charge of that, Tunch. You're going to have to ask Tom O'Malley." I called him and said, "T.O., can I play on the basketball team? Please. I'm out of money." I mean, I was begging him. Thankfully he said, "Tunch, I can get you on early." Meanwhile, Billy Hurley said, "Let's you and me rent a house." We found a house in Bethel Park, but I still didn't know if I would have enough money. He said, "Listen, I'll front the first month. You pay me as we start making money for basketball."

The first weekend that basketball started none of the veterans were in town, and there were only six of us. The pot was bigger to split, and we played a game on Friday night, a game on Saturday night, and two games on Sunday. I made almost enough money to pay for the next three months' rent. I played that whole offseason because I was there and dependable. It was great because you got your running in and you got out in the community.

We had a great hoops team: Cliff Stoudt, Jimmy Smith, Theo Bell, and Larry "Bubba" Brown. Those guys all looked like college basketball players. I was nowhere near those guys. Hurley could play, and Bobby could play. Courson could dunk at 6'1", 275 pounds. The funny thing is he couldn't take off on one foot. He would have a breakaway and he would plant both feet before dunking. It was insane. He was a beast and he could do a 360 dunk. He was an amazing athlete and he also ran a 4.7-second 40-yard dash time.

The Steelers didn't work out at the facility, and Jon Kolb, Mike Webster, Bubba, and Courson all trained at the Red Bull Inn on Route 19. It wasn't a great gym, but it had a squat rack, a bench, a pulley machine, dumbbells, and a pull-up machine. I started training with those guys every morning, and it was really tough because those guys were so much stronger than I was.

I didn't want to take too many 45-pound plates off the bar and I actually hurt my back squatting too much. But those guys really took me under their wing. We trained together and after we had finished I would go eat this giant breakfast. I was small and had trouble keeping weight on. I ate eggs, cheeseburgers, french fries. As the weather started getting nicer, Courson and I played pick-up basketball at South Park after we got done lifting. That whole offseason was the same thing.

Minicamp came around, and it was still kind of touch-and-go with me. I was definitely a bubble guy. I was so excited to see Wolf, who was up to around 285 pounds. We decided to room together and we got really, really close. His dad had leukemia and was really sick, so his mom and dad would come in, and I got to know them, especially his mom. To this day she prays for my children and grandchildren.

I was really nervous in training camp because I didn't think I was going to make the team. I had the stomach jitters and in the middle of practice I would start ralphing a little bit and everybody would say, "Ohh, Tunch! What's wrong with you?" Huddles are usually tight, but because I was standing there throwing up, nobody would get near me. Chuck would yell, "Tighten up that huddle! Tighten up that huddle!" They would say, "No way! He's puking."

I used that to my advantage in a preseason game. We played the Cleveland Browns, which was really unusual since they were in our division, and they had a nose tackle named Ron Simmons. He had played at Florida State and he was a guy who liked to crowd the ball. I was playing center, and my stomach was flip-flopping in the huddle. We came up to the line of scrimmage for a play, and all of the sudden, I threw up. He stood up, and we came off the ball. Wolf and I were on a double team, and we just took him out. He said, "You're sick!" And Wolf said, "Yeah, he's been sick all camp."

Wolf's Words

 Tunch was sure he was going to get cut that preseason, even though he was playing well. He just had this nervous stomach. About halfway through practice, he would start gurgling a little and at some point he would start throwing up, and it was not a little bit. It came gushing out. In the second half against Cleveland, Tunch played center for Mike Webster, and I was at left guard. Cliff Stoudt was the quarterback, and he called a *Toss 33 Trap*, where Tunch and I doubled teamed Ron Simmons. As Stoudt called the play in the huddle, I heard Tunch making these gurgling noises and I said, "Uh oh."

We started to jog toward the line of scrimmage, and I heard Tunch wretch and I just kind of swerved a little to my left. We got to the line of scrimmage, and Stoudt was looking over the defense. Simmons was in a four-point stance and he was just within whiskers of Tunch. We went down into our three-point stance, and at the snap of the ball, two things simultaneously happened: Tunch snapped the ball back into Stoudt's hands, and violently vomited into the face of Simmons. It came out like a fire hose. While he was vomiting and launching into Simmons, I was coming down on a double team to his hip. You know how you grab your face if someone just threw something in your eyes? Simmons stood up and screamed with both hands, and we pushed him like 15 yards down the field. We just crushed him. It was the best double team you had ever seen in your life. We slammed him to the ground, and when we got up, he was spitting vomit out of his mouth. He said, "You're sick!" Tunch turned and vomited on my foot. He said to Simmons, "You're right."

We got back to the huddle, and I stood to Tunch's right, and we had our backs to the line of scrimmage. I stood about two feet away from him, and everybody was in a normal position, not knowing what just occurred except for Stoudt, who watched the whole thing. Stoudt said, "How much pregame did you eat, Tunch, because I think we should run that one again." The next time Simmons was in over Tunch, he played like three yards off the ball. Even funnier is after that series Chuck started yelling at me as we came to the sidelines because I had left a gap in the huddle. He said, "Wolf, you've got to understand they're reading Stoudt's lips" because Stoudt was right across Tunch in the huddle, and you could see him talk if I wasn't in my normal spot. He said, "Bunch it up." I said, "I would, but Tunch chunked on my foot, coach." Tunch came walking by, and Chuck said, "What?" Almost if on command, Tunch threw up, and it nearly landed on Chuck, who said, "Oh, okay."

Wolf was a full-time starter by his second season, and I made the team as a backup. We kept 10 offensive linemen that year, and I could play center, guard, and tackle. I was also on all of the special teams. My rookie year I had played on all of the special teams and I don't want this to sound like bragging, but I was a good special teams player. I was light at 245, 250 pounds and I could run. You would get a point for a tackle and a point for a block and my first two years I led the special teams in points. That's where I made my bones.

My rookie year I didn't get on the field as an offensive lineman. Not once. My second year I got some playing time. In short-yardage and goal line, Ray Pinney moved to tight end, and I came in and played his left tackle spot. I then got one extra play because he had to go out before he could come back in at an ineligible receiving position (after being eligible).

I did anything I could to get on the field that second season—and stay there. We were in Seattle in early November, and I was in at left tackle after Ray Pinney moved to tight end for a play. Ray had to stay out for one more play before coming back in at left tackle, and Wolf got jacked on that play. He was lying on the ground with a hip pointer, and an idea hit me. I said, "I think you should go out. That looks bad." I was the backup center and tackle, but Ricky Donnalley was the backup guard. After talking Wolf into going out, I stayed in at guard, and Ricky said, "Wait a second! How come he's in?" Mike Webster said, "You staying?" I said, "Yeah, I'm going to make them grab me." It turned out to be a great move because I found out from Kolby later that Chuck loved that I wouldn't come out.

Chuck didn't like what happened after we got fogged in and stayed in Seattle that night. We went to this cowboy bar called Montana's and stayed there too long. They were trying to kick us out, and on the way out Gary Dunn, Courson, and I were hitting this punching bag and it was going straight back. Stoudt said, "Out of my way" and roundhoused it and broke his wrist. He crumpled to the ground and said, "I think I broke my wrist." We all laughed, thinking he was joking. If that wasn't enough, the manager had called Chuck and said, "Your team is here and they won't leave." The next morning defensive line coach George Perles came in and said, "You guys better get your story straight because Chuck is on the warpath." Rollie Dotsch, our offensive line coach, said, "I don't care if we go by packed mule and canoe, we will never stay overnight after a game again."

Chuck never asked us about it; he just yelled at us. He said in the team meeting room, "I've never been so ashamed of a team. We lose our quarterback to a punching bag. The whole team had to be asked to leave an establishment and they wouldn't. And apparently one of us was so intoxicated we couldn't find the urinal." (I actually remember the culprit, but I don't want to embarrass the guy.)

Things started looking up for me when I saw more extended action because of an injury. It happened after Bubba hurt his hamstring against the Los Angeles Rams at Three Rivers Stadium. I went in at right tackle and I was playing against Jack Youngblood. Terry Bradshaw said, "You ready, Hoss?" I was nervous as all get out. *I've got to block Jack Youngblood? Oh my gosh!* And I lied through my teeth, I said, "I'm ready to roll, buddy. I'm ready to roll." He said, "C'mon, let's go have some fun." I ended up playing well against Youngblood, and we beat the Rams 24–0.

The next week we went to Oakland for *Monday Night Football*, and it was supposed to be my first start and I had to play against the Raiders' John Matuszak, who was 6'7", 280 pounds. I started getting nervous on Wednesday and on the flight out to Oakland all I could think about was hearing Howard's voice: *A typ-ical rook-ie mis-take by the young man from Turkey.* I just thought he was going to have a field day with my name and the fact that I was the first Turkey native to play in the NFL. I never really thought much about it, though I got asked about it often early in my career.

My folks lived in San Francisco, and Gary Dunn, John Goodman, and I went to their house for a big Turkish dinner on Sunday night. Turkish hamburgers are called *kofte* and they are made from a spicy, garlicy ground meat. They are like small sausages and they are really good. We had those as well as a garlic cucumber sauce, rice pilaf, *manti*, which is Turkish ravioli, and a cold bean dish. It was all my favorite stuff, and I couldn't even eat because I was so nervous. J.R.—we always called Goodman that—and Dunny were just chowing down, and I was just like, "Okay, let's go back to the hotel."

Before that Raiders game, Bubba said, "Let me see if I can give this a try." He went out there for one maybe two plays and he couldn't do it; he re-injured his hamstring. He said, "Tunch, you can do this. You're going to be all right. Just keep punching, just keep punching." He watched me all game and said, "You're doing great, you're doing great. Just keep punching, keep punching." I played well, and what was cool about that was guys like Kolby, Webby, Wolf, Bubba, Courson, and Franco Harris were so supportive.

After that game I thought I could play in the league. If that Oakland game was a turning point in my career, the flight home was when Webby asked me a question that ultimately changed my life. "Tunch," he said, "if you died today, where would you spend eternity?"

Steelers 1980 NFL Draft Class

Round	Player/Position	College	Overall Selection
1	Mark Malone/QB	Arizona State	28
2	Bob Kohrs/LB	Arizona State	35
2	John Goodman/DE	Oklahoma	56
3	Ray Sydnor/TE	Wisconsin	83
4	Bill Hurley/QB	Syracuse	110
5	Craig Wolfley/G	Syracuse	138
6	**Tunch Ilkin/C**	**Indiana State**	**165**
7	Nate Johnson/WR	Hillsdale	193
8	Ted Walton/DB	Connecticut	221
9	Ron McCall/WR	Arkansas Pine-Bluff	249
10	Woodrow Wilson/DB	N.C. State	250
10	Ken Fritz/G	Ohio State	277
11	Frank Pollard/RB	Baylor	305
12	Charles Vaclavik/DB	Texas	306
12	Tyrone McGriff/G	Florida A&M	333

CHAPTER 8

The Crucible of Camp

I hated training camp as a player, absolutely hated it. After the last day of camp, we got on Route 30 in Latrobe, Pennsylvania, drove home, and it seemed like the rest of the season went faster than the six weeks we spent in training camp. Training camp was so different than it is now.

I remember the first time the Steelers went to a movie when Bill Cowher was the head coach to give the players a break from camp. I said, "We never went to a movie. We never had popsicle breaks. We didn't have these Jacuzzis." We never had golf carts either. We walked everywhere at St. Vincent College, and fans were allowed on campus then, so you signed autographs the whole time you were walking. These guys have it so easy. Defensive lineman Chris Hoke once said, "Our camp is hard." I said, "Your camp is hard? Are you kidding me? Give me a break. Try having a two-a-days for two-and-a-half weeks. Try having two-and-a-half-hour practices."

Back then second and sometimes even third-year players had to come in two weeks early with the rookies. I had to do that my first two years, I think. The third year Craig Wolfley and I were nervous because we thought we were going to be called in. I called Wolf's house one day, and his wife answered. I said, "Hi, this is Chuck Noll. We need Craig to come in early." He got on the phone eventually, and I said, "Hey, we need you up here," and then I started laughing.

Wolf's Words

 My first wife answered the phone, and I had been trying to explain to her not to answer the phone after rookie camp started. *How do you not answer the phone all week long?* She picked up the phone one day, and it was Tunch, and he fooled her by imitating Coach Noll. I had been warning her that I did not want to go to camp early, and she turned to me and had this look of horror in her eyes. I was mad at her for picking up the phone and now I was even madder. I was gritting my teeth, and my heart rate just accelerated. I took the phone and I wasn't really listening because I was so mad and I was trying to think of some way I could excuse myself from having to go to camp during double practices and in a heat wave that had engulfed Pittsburgh. I heard a voice and said, "Yes, Coach," and something went off in my head within seconds that something wasn't quite right, but I believed it was Coach Noll. Tunch went on for probably no more than 20 seconds and then he started cracking up. I exploded because I was so mad and then realized I was getting pranked yet again. I was yelling at the phone and I'm sure I used strong language back then. I was very angry with my Turkish brother.

We didn't have cellphones, and there were no phones in the dorm rooms during training camp. You fought over the payphones on the floor, and there was no air conditioning. Camp was hot and physical, and every day your manhood was challenged. Pranking each other helped keep us sane, though one time it almost caused Jack Lambert to lose his mind.

Defensive lineman Tom Beasley and Lambert were really good buddies and they always pranked one another. Tom came up with the best gag pulled on anyone in all my years of training camp. Tom had a buddy come to camp and he brought a rattlesnake with him in this box. We went to practice, and Tom's buddy got ready to leave, but before he did, he put the rattlesnake in another box. He gave the box that we all saw the rattlesnake in to Tom after everyone else had left. Tom took it to his room and kept it there. That night everybody went out after meetings, and Tom put that open box in Jack's room. Mike Webster also took a giant black rubber snake and put it under Jack's pillow. At camp the veterans were on the first floor, and the rookies were on the second floor, but Jack—the recluse that he was—stayed on the third floor by himself.

Jack came back at around 10:45 PM, and all of the sudden we heard, "ATTEMPTED MURDERER! ATTEMPTED MURDERER! BEASLEY, YOU'RE GOING TO JAIL!" He was screaming this at the top of his lungs, so we went running up to his room. Chuck heard it and he came up to the third floor, too. Chuck, who was playing the ukulele, was in kicker Matt Bahr's room when all of this happened. I busted on Matt later, "Oh, you and Chuck had a jam session?"

As Jack was going off, Tom walked down the hall in his sleeping shorts and cowboy boots. Tom said, "Jack, just put on some cowboy boots. They can't strike any higher than your calf." Jack went nuts again. He was yelling, "YOU'RE GOING TO JAIL, BEAS! ATTEMPTED MURDERER. I'M GOING TO FILE A COMPLAINT!"

Jack Lambert was an intimidating presence, but that didn't stop his teammates from pranking him during training camp.

Noll said, "Relax, Jack. What's wrong?"

He said, "ATTEMPTED MURDERER! BEASLEY'S TRYING TO KILL ME! LOOK AT THAT! THERE'S A RATTLESNAKE IN MY ROOM!"

Chuck said, "How do you know there's a rattlesnake in your room?" Chuck started walking into the room, and Jack said, "Because this afternoon there was a rattlesnake in that box, and now that box is empty in my room!"

Chuck then backed up. That morning the league had come in and said if you had an alcohol or drug problem, you could get help, and the coaches didn't even have to know about it. Beasley said, "Don't worry, Jack, there's places for people like you. And the coaches don't even have to know." Lambert finally cooled down, and Beasley said, "Oh, come on. You know it's just a gag."

Everybody broke up, and we went back to our rooms. Lambert got into bed, put his hand under the pillow, and found the rubber snake. Then he started screaming, and everybody else started cracking up.

We had different gags at camp, including one we called "the mongoose," which was a box with a tail. Gary Dunn started it and he willed it to me after he retired. He would tell guys, "Hey, my buddy's got a mongoose and I'm thinking about bringing it. Mongooses are cool. We'll feed it stuff. It's fun to watch. It will eat snakes. It will eat chicken."

My third or fourth year, Wolf and I roomed together, and it was the congregating room because we were the first ones to bust open the window and put a wall air-conditioning unit in the window. Wolf had brought a 10,000 BTU window unit air conditioner, which is for a ballroom. We broke the window—not shattered it—but broke the frame. We duct taped that sucker in there and we put towels around it so it fit in the window. You turned that thing on, and there would eventually be frost on our walls.

Everybody called our room the meat locker, and guys would come in and watch TV and play cards.

When Dunny brought the mongoose to camp for the first time, we told everyone to come to our room later. The box was three-feet long, so you could get into half of the box, and it was covered with barbed wire and had the tail sticking out of it. It was a racoon tail that was spring-loaded. We would put in chicken bones and rib bones in the box like it could eat that stuff, and guys would watch. Dunny would then release the lock, and the top popped open, and that little fur tail came flying out. It scared the crap out of guys. Defensive lineman Keith Willis once knocked about three people over, knocked a dresser over, and ran down the hallway yelling, "The mongoose is loose, the mongoose is loose!" We got Joe Greene when he was a rookie coach with the Steelers. He ran out of the room initially. That is the only time I've seen him scared. It was so funny.

Camp itself was anything but a joke. You reported on a Thursday and you went down on the field in shorts and T-shirts and did your 40-yard dash test and then the conditioning test. When I was a rookie, the conditioning test was five 350-yard runs. You had to do them in a minute and 10 seconds and you had a minute and 10 seconds to rest between each one. And we did those every other day after the second practice of each day. The next morning after the conditioning test you were in pads, and the very first thing you did after individual drills was the Oklahoma drill.

Chuck believed it set the tone for camp since it was essentially one-on-one blocking and tackling drills. There were three lines, and everybody watched. You were nervous because the TV cameras were up on the hillside. Chuck did the drill right there for everybody to see, and my rookie year he said, "Today is the day to earn the respect of your peers."

If all of that wasn't enough, I spent extra time with Chuck early in my career, trying to learn how to long snap. Morning practices ended at about 11:00, and I stayed until about 11:30. My first two years I was with Chuck because he was the long-snapping coach and he could actually long snap. He would say, "Make your arms like spaghetti. You're too tense. You're too tense." He spent all of this time with me after practice because he was such a teacher.

Long snapping, I believe to this day, is a knack, and you either have it or you don't. I did not have it. I wanted to get good at it, but I wasn't seeing any light at the end of the tunnel. But I was working with Chuck, so I wasn't going to say, "Okay, I've had enough."

Camp always had stress; it was—like the heat at St. Vincent College—measured in degrees. You approached every play like it was your last one because you knew you were always being evaluated. Whatever you did that day, you knew you were going to watch it that night with the coaches. Chuck put a huge emphasis on winning every battle, so there was never any let up. There was such intensity every day at practice.

In 1984, a year after we lost in the playoffs to the Los Angeles Raiders and stunk in that game, I endured the hardest camp of my career. We called it the "Purge of '84." Ricky Donnalley got traded, Steve Courson got traded, a bunch of guys got cut. Camp was so hard that year that we started saying, "What's the worst thing they could do? They could keep you."

In training camp things get so boring that guys would do anything to break up the monotony. That's what Ricky was doing. He wrapped his face in a semi-transparent wrap as a gag, and Chuck walked in and initially did not take it as a gag. He said, "Take. That. Off." But then Chuck tried to inject a little humor and said, "Whoa! Put it back on."

If they cut or traded you that camp, they said they wanted to see you behind the curtain. It happened to Ricky, and he was gone. He didn't come out. If you went behind the curtain you got sucked into the vortex and never returned. Steve was the only one who came out from behind the curtain. He said, "Tampa Bay, guys! I'm out of here! Yeah, Daddy!" And he just walked out.

We were on the field for the second practice, and all of the sudden he was driving in his tricked-out Blazer and he was blasting Hank Williams, Jr. real loud. He was honking, and everybody was waving. That was one of the most memorable exits I've ever seen.

Steve was a character, and one camp he and Dunny were doing triceps extensions in their room to see who could do more. Steve did like 25. Dunny got up there and he was up to 23 or 24 and thought he was going to break Steve's record. He got to 25 and he needed just one more. All of the sudden, Chuck, who hated bodybuilding, walked into the room. He was standing over Gary, who was on the ground, and said, "What are we doing, Gary? Bodybuilding?" That just took the wind right out of Dunny's sails. The next day Chuck said to defensive coordinator Woody Widenhofer, "Are we working these guys hard enough?" Woody said, "Gee, Chuck, we're working them plenty hard. Why do you ask?" Noll said, "I walked into Dunny's room last night. He and Steve were drunk as shit and they were bodybuilding."

As tough as camp was, guys always found a way to, as Chuck would say, replenish their body fluids. The best part of the day was after the second practice. Sometimes we went to a place called the Inn-termission to get a beer and something to turn on our appetite because you didn't feel like eating right away. We went to the Inn-termission or the 19th Hole, another nearby bar, and it was just the guys.

Mike Wagner, Jack Ham, and Moon Mullins took Billy Hurley, Bobby Kohrs, and John Goodman to the 19th Hole one time my rookie year. I was getting treatment so I couldn't go. I was waiting at the bottom of the steps when those guys came in, and they were just a little bit tipsy. Chuck was standing there, and they all passed him. Chuck said, "You better be careful who you associate with because it tells a lot about you."

Some guys would go to different bars, but Wolf and I always went to Bull's Tavern. The young guys, who weren't married or didn't have significant others, would go out looking for women. Us married guys just wanted to be out and we had so much fun at Bull's Tavern.

It was great because not a lot of people went there and it was like our own little bar. There was always air conditioning, and Bull Turnbull was the greatest guy. He had been a policeman in McKeesport, Pennsylvania, and the way we discovered Bull's was through a buddy of mine from Indiana State, Gerry Glusic, who was from McKeesport.

He was friends with Bull's son, Tommy Turnbull, and the summer before my rookie year Gerry said, "Why don't you come into Pittsburgh and live with me and my parents and we can work out together?" Gerry had signed with the Steelers as an undrafted free agent so I lived in McKeesport with him and his family. We went to the McKeesport YMCA and ran at McKeesport High School. One day we went to this place called Lake Stoughton on Route 30, and Gerry said, "You know my buddy's dad just bought a bar out here. I think that's it."

We stopped in, and that's how I met Bull. We went there during rookie camp when we had a free minute. Bull would bring out this big platter of frog legs and we would have a couple of beers and would throw darts, shoot pool, and play Space Invaders and Pac-Man. We had about an hour before we had to jump into the car and speed back to camp to get in before curfew.

Not that curfews or bed checks stopped guys from sneaking out. In my day we called it going "over the wall." There wasn't a literal wall, but we always referred to breaking curfew as going over the wall. We would sneak out the back door of the dorm and go up over the cemetery where we had parked our cars in a side lot and drive off. The first time I went over the wall it was with John, Gary, and Wolf. We were sneaking out and all of the sudden we saw running backs coach Dick Hoak in the parking lot. We started running down the hill to the door, and John fell and rolled down the hill. I thought he blew out his knee. Hoakie went into the beer room, where the coaches would hang out, so we went back out.

I wasn't a guy who liked to go out, but the challenge of going over the wall was the whole reason for doing it. You didn't really want to go over the wall much because you were so tired and wanted to get enough sleep. It got to a point where going over the wall was once a year. It was a tradition, and so Wolf and I always did it. The last year that Wolf was with the Steelers we were so tired, but we were like, "C'mon, we've got to do it." We went over the wall, went through the drive-thru at Wendy's, and came back. But it was the principle. We did it.

There wasn't a lot to do at night when we got back to our dorm rooms after position-group meetings, and it was just a different time. I remember how great we thought it was when a Subway sandwich shop came to Latrobe. Before cable TV everyone read books and we passed all of these spy novels around. That's how I became a Jason Bourne fan. I read all of Robert Ludlum's books. I mean, I read them all. You would be in our beds at like 11:00 and you didn't want to go to sleep because you knew the whole process was going to start all over again, like it was Groundhog's Day. You would say, "No, I don't want to go to sleep, I don't want to go to sleep." You eventually fell asleep, and when you woke up the next morning, it took a long time to get moving because you were so tired from this dead sleep. You went to breakfast, went to put our pads on, and then went to the 9:00 AM meeting. You were on the field at 9:30 and practiced until 11:30.

After going to lunch, you tried not to sleep afterwards because if you took a nap, you were going to wake up groggy. But you were so tired that you would lay down. The next thing you knew, we'd be out. The alarm would go off at 2:00 PM, and we would start putting your pads on because you did that in your room before trudging down to the practice fields. Waking up in the mornings felt even worse if you couldn't see the mountains because of the mist. You called that "hold on to your ass" day because the heat and humidity were going to kill you. The air just sat in that valley, where the fields were, and you felt like you could get a drink of water right out of the air. That's how heavy the air was.

Camp was simply awful. On Saturdays after practice, we were off at 5:00 PM until Sunday at 6:00 PM. We had to be back for dinner and then the 7:00 PM meeting. That 24 hours was like the greatest 24 hours in the world. I just went home and watched TV. I sat there and said, "Oh, I don't want to go back. Don't make me go back." Sharon always joked, "Do you want me to write you a note? Dear Chuck, please excuse Tunch from practice."

Chuck beat us up for two weeks of camp, and then we'd be done with it. But even after that, we had a morning walkthrough and we still had a really tough second practice. As grueling and as exhausting as camp was, I think it helped safeguard us from some the injuries you see frequently today. The two-a-days during camp and three padded practices a week during the season meant we were always going hard. In that sense I think what the NFL Players Association has done recently to try to protect players has actually hurt them. You didn't hear of nearly as many ACL tears in my day. Guys are tearing ACLs left and right these days, and a lot of them are non-contact. We had a couple of ACL tears, but today they happen all of the time. Torn triceps. Torn biceps. Did you ever hear of that? No, and I think that's because we went hard all of the time. At the time I thought it was going to hurt my longevity, but in retrospect it was the reason we didn't get hurt as much.

My perspective of St. Vincent has totally changed now that I go there for my radio show with Wolf and watch practices instead of participate in them. Now that I am not a player, I can really admire and appreciate the beauty up there, the surrounding hills of the Laurel Highlands. I get up every morning and I walk. I love walking and praying. I walk around the cemetery and around campus. It's a really great environment for training camp, and I understand why Mike Tomlin likes it. He likes the guys together, and there is a chemistry that happens in camp.

I love going up there, especially since it is a place that reflects the Rooneys' faith, family, football. Wolf and I have a cigar every night before dinner because it is the perfect time. It is right at dusk, and the day is done. Art Rooney II came up to us one time and said, "Oh, I didn't know this was part of the itinerary." A couple of days later, I saw him, and he was talking to one of the other owners. I said, "Hey, we're going to be up there after practice if you want to come have a cigar." I didn't think he was going to come, but he did. We sat there and talked about his dad and stories from when he was a ballboy.

Art's a great guy and he told the story of when he and scout Bill Nunn's son stole Joe Greene's car. They went to Pittsburgh, visited their friends, came back before dinner, and put the car back. I said, "Hey, Art, I'm impressed. Any ballboy who can steal Joe Greene's car and live to tell about it, I'm impressed with that." He said, "He never found out until way, way later."

Training camp and St. Vincent have produced so many funny stories like that one.

And camp is the only time I saw Chuck speechless. It happened after the field-goal team went out for a kick during practice. Punter Harry Newsome, the holder, fumbled the snap, and kicker Gary Anderson went out in the flat. Harry threw a pass to Gary, and linebacker Tyronne Stowe lit him up. He knocked out our kicker's two front teeth, and Anderson was laid out. Noll stopped and didn't say anything. Everybody was standing around, and nobody was saying anything, and all of their jaws had dropped. Finally, I said, "Okay, move the drill!" That was because if someone got hurt Chuck would always say, "Okay, let's move the drill." But Chuck was really affected by Tyronne's hit. I was thinking to myself, *He wasn't that upset when I blew out my elbow.* Tyronne said, "Good-bye, guys. I'm gone." But he didn't actually get cut nor should he have because he was just reacting like a football player. And as for Gary, he spit out two Chicklets but he didn't miss any time. You can kick with no teeth.

CHAPTER 9

Tunch Punch

I met Ryan Harris, an offensive tackle who had just signed with the Steelers, in 2016 and said, "Hi, I'm Tunch Ilkin. Welcome to Pittsburgh." He said, "Hi, I'm Ryan Harris. What's your name?" I said, "Tunch Ilkin." He said, "*Tunch Punch?*" I said, "I guess I've been called that." He said, "That's *you?* Wow, we did your stuff in college!" I get that reaction every once in a while. It's kind of crazy, and I don't know how to respond.

Joe Greene and I were at a banquet together at Steelers' fantasy camp in June of 2017, and he said, "Tunch, what happened when I told you how to recoil your hands and punch?" I said, "I don't know." He said, "You became Tunch Punch."

Tunch Punch—I never call myself that—took a little from here, a little from there, starting with Joe and Jon Kolb, one of my mentors with the Steelers and an anchor on the offensive line in the 1970s. I watched Kolby punch Dwight White in one-on-one drills my rookie year. I went to him and said, "How did you do that?" He said, "Do you ever watch westerns?" I said, "Yeah." He said, "Do you like the quick draw?" I said, "I love it." He said, "It's the same thing. Get your hands up quick and pop him in the chest." I said, "Well, show me." He said, "Brace yourself," and then he hit me. It felt like the paddles in ER. After that I watched Kolby all of the time because I knew I was never going to get on the field as a center, even though I was drafted as one. I thought maybe I could get on the field as a backup guard, tackle, something.

It made a lot of sense to me so I followed Kolby around. He was always very welcoming, and I really got to know him and become friends with him when he became the strength coach after he retired in 1982. When I gave my life to Christ in February of 1982, Kolby was real excited. I started going to Bible study at Kolby's house, and he mentored me as a man of God and as an offensive lineman. He showed me how to train.

The veterans helping younger guys is a special thing with the Steelers. We had a very special mentoring philosophy because Chuck Noll was such

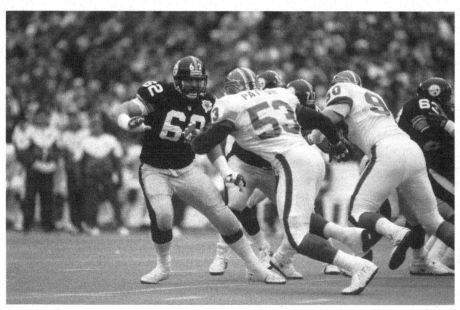

I ready to block Buffalo Bills linebacker Marvcus Patton and perhaps use the "Tunch Punch," a move for which I became known. (Pittsburgh Steelers)

122

a teacher. He was always teaching, always tinkering, and so we realized we need to be teaching one another. Early in my career, when I backed up Larry Brown, he always said, "Watch me. Watch my technique. Make sure I punch. Watch my steps."

I made progress under such tutelage and became a full-time starter in 1983. It was kind of a crazy year. Ray Pinney had left, and Ted Petersen and I were competing to be the starting left tackle. I had a great offseason, but right before camp, I was bench pressing and tore my rotator cuff. I probably got hurt more in the weight room than I ever did on the football field because I lifted with Craig Wolfley, Mike Webster, Larry "Bubba" Brown, and Kolby. I tried to keep up with them, but my tendons were just not that strong and I got real bad tendinitis. I once tore a pec—I still have the hole—bench pressing and I hurt my rotator cuff because I was benching too much weight.

I got to camp and tried to play but had no luck. The Steelers put me on the four-week injured reserve to let it rest. I came back in Week 5, and Bubba got hurt in my second week back so I became the starting right tackle. I played really well at first and was feeling good. But I got the flu and I couldn't lift because my shoulder was messed up. My weight dropped. I missed the Detroit Lions game, and my flu was so bad that I was quarantined the night before the game.

Ted broke his foot in that game, and with Bubba back in the lineup, I moved over to left tackle.

It was great playing full time, and we started 9–2 that season with Cliff Stoudt as our quarterback. All of the sudden, we hit a bad stretch and lost three games in a row. We needed to defeat the New York Jets on a Saturday afternoon in the last game at Shea Stadium. Terry Bradshaw hadn't thrown a ball in a year because of offseason elbow surgery, but he replaced Stoudt for this game. The Jets had the famed New York Sack Exchange of Joe Klecko, Marty Lyons, Abdul Salaam, and Mark Gastineau.

Terry came into the huddle on our opening possession with the biggest smile you ever saw and said, "C'mon, boys, let's have some fun!" He just started throwing the ball all over the field. He threw a touchdown pass to Calvin Sweeney, and we got the ball back. He threw another touchdown pass and then he was done forever. He tore up a bunch of scar tissue that game but made quite an exit in leading us to a 34–7 win that clinched a playoff berth. I was sitting next to him on the bench at one point during the game and I said, "Damn, Terry. I thought we were going to run the ball." He said, "Tunch, you know me. I ain't no mailman, I'm a gunslinger." I said, "That you are."

Stoudt had been getting booed really bad at home, and at Shea Stadium there were two or three Richard Todd dolls hanging in effigy. I was sitting next to Stoudt and I said, "See that? At least they're not hanging you."

The place went crazy afterward because it was the last game at Shea Stadium, and Lyons had warned us to keep our helmets on. It was just like what happened at Three Rivers Stadium almost a decade later. People ran onto the field and pulled out stadium seats for souvenirs. A cop dragged one guy away for fighting while Chuck was doing a live postgame interview with NBC. This guy was cussing, but when he saw Chuck, he said, "Hey, nice game, Coach."

We played the Los Angeles Raiders in the divisional round of the playoffs and we spent the entire week before the game in California. Our practices were brutal, and we just killed each other. It was like training camp. My weight was down to 240 pounds, and I was down to benching 135 pounds because of my bad shoulder. I was terrible that day, and we lost 38–10. I gave up three sacks against Lyle Alzado. That game haunts me to this day.

We got back to Pittsburgh, and everything I read said Tunch Ilkin sucks. Stan Savran, a Pittsburgh radio legend and now a colleague of mine, said the Steelers will never win with me at tackle. That whole offseason I vowed that kind of performance would never happen again. As depressing as it was, I played really well the first eight games of that season. My confidence wasn't shot.

That offseason I started training at the Pennsylvania Karate Academy, and met Bill Edwards. He became a pivotal figure in my development. Everyone called him "Sarge," and he was one of the greatest martial artists that I've ever seen. He had trained with some of Bruce Lee's pupils and at 6'0", 180 pounds could kick the rim on a basketball hoop. Sarge was just unbelievable.

He had seen me working out and said, "What are you trying to accomplish?" I said, "I want to be a better football player." He said, "Well, if you keep working out like that, you're just going to be a better martial artist. If you want to be a better football player, why don't you come train with me?" I thought that was very intriguing. Although he was not a football guy, he understood what we were trying to accomplish.

I told him I was trying to jam and punch defenders when they throw their pass rush move. The goal was to stop him and make him redirect or restart. I wanted to stop the initial move and then stop the counter move. We started using a little bit of what is called *Wing Chun*, which is trapping the hands, and then Sarge did this thing called sticky hands, and it was how you got your hands back on the guy really quick. It also generated enough open-handed force to really rattle a guy's cage when you cranked him. Foundationally, it is martial arts and it's centered on hard placement and torque.

It was a workout, and I would tell Sarge what worked and what didn't. Wolf and I were kind of his guinea pigs. Different guys—like Wolf, Pete

Rostosky, and Terry Long—jumped in and worked out with us, but I was obsessed with this. I was with Sarge every offseason except the year I had both of my shoulders fixed, and it really helped develop my pass protection skills.

Going into camp in 1984, I felt great—until the business of the game intruded. I didn't have a contract, and my agent told one of the Pittsburgh newspapers, "If Tunch doesn't get a contract, he'll just go to the USFL." The headline said, "Tunch Ilkin threatens to go to the USFL." I had no idea he was going to say that. The first game at Three Rivers I got booed. Fortunately, that didn't prove to be an omen. All of the sudden, it clicked for me. The lightbulb went on, and I had my best season from an individual and team standpoint.

We went to the AFC Championship Game, and I got better and better as the season progressed. We played the Raiders the last game of the season, and the media was saying, "Tunch, last year you played against Lyle Alzado and you stunk up the joint. This year you're playing against Howie Long, who's a lot better." I said, "I'm just going to do my best." I played really well that game, and that may have been my most memorable season as a player. We beat the Raiders 13–7 and got into the playoffs with a 9–7 record after the two teams we needed to lose their last game did just that.

We played a divisional playoff game at Denver, and that season the Broncos had so many takeaways. Webby said, "They have a transition game like the Boston Celtics so don't turn the ball over." The first two plays of the game we fumbled. We were walking off the field after the second fumble, and Wolf and I looked at each other and said, "Plan B?" But the defense held the Raiders to three combined points after those two turnovers, and we won the game with a takeaway of our own when Gary Dunn intercepted a middle screen pass. That place had been rocking, and fans had been yelling, "Bring on Marino! Bring on the

Dolphins!" By the end of the game, you could have heard a pin drop. It was so quiet.

I went up against Doug Betters, the NFL Defensive Player of the Year, in the AFC Championship Game in Miami. He headslapped me one play, and I cussed him out. He said, "I can't help it. You're so short." So, I punched him in the face. The first half was close, but in the second half, Dan Marino went crazy. I didn't know he was that good. I really thought we were going to beat the Dolphins, but he threw so many long touchdown passes to Mark Clayton and Mark Duper. One time the defense was walking off the field, and Webby said, "Can you just slow them down a little?" I held my own against Betters, and Hal Hunter, who was with the Colts before coming to Pittsburgh as an assistant line coach in 1985, later said, "I've never seen anyone play Doug Betters that well."

One thing that was crucial to my development happened after the '84 season. Ron Blackledge, our offensive line coach, said, "How can I help you get better?" I said, "Just keep me at one position." He said, "I think I can do that." When you play center, guard, and tackle in the early part of your development, it helps you because you understand the offense. You get better because you experience what it means to play the left side versus the right side, guard versus tackle, center versus guard. But then it comes to a point where it starts slowing your development because you need to play one position. I said, "Just put me at one side, whether it's right or left. I don't care."

I had flipped between left and right tackle because Larry was near the end of his career, and he got hurt a lot. Playing left tackle had been difficult because I had never done it before coming to the Steelers. I think left tackle is hard if you're not left-handed because you play better to the side you open your stance to, and the angle is better. If you're always used to playing out of a left-handed stance with your left foot behind your right one, it becomes natural. But if you've always been in a right-handed stance, it's like playing golf left-handed. It is that foreign.

I realized if I was going to play left tackle, I had to play out of a left-handed stance, and it was a lot of work. I started eating left-handed. Every time I ran a sprint I did it from a left-handed stance. I tried to do everything left handed, so I could feel comfortable on that side.

Then Ray returned to the Steelers after his stint in the USFL and settled in at left tackle. I exclusively became a right tackle following Larry's retirement. After 1984 I never played left tackle again. I liked playing right tackle better and I started coming into my own once I found a permanent home there.

In 1986 I think I gave up one sack and in '87 I gave up no sacks in a strike-shortened season. I got a call from Jim McNally, the offensive line coach for the Cincinnati Bengals, and he said, "Tunch, you should have been in the Pro Bowl this year. You got jobbed." Chuck had said, "Tunch, keep working hard because I want to be able to vote for you for the Pro Bowl." I thought, *Wow, what integrity.* Also, that was such an affirmation because he said I was almost good enough for him to vote for me.

After the '87 season, I made the *Sports Illustrated* All-Pro team. The day the Pro Bowl was announced in 1988, I saw Chuck, and he said, "Congratulations, Tunch, you're going to the Pro Bowl." I called Sharon when I found out about it, and she started crying. I didn't know what to do at the press conference or what to say. I forget who asked me—it might have been Ed Bouchette or John Clayton—but he said, "Tunch, the Steelers haven't missed sending a guy to the Pro Bowl in the last 20 years, and if you didn't make the Pro Bowl, they would have missed this year." I thought, *I'm sure glad the Steelers are sending someone to the Pro Bowl this year and I'm sure glad it's me.*

After that Stan Savran did a piece on me, and he wrote "Outside Three Rivers Stadium there is a statue to consistency, hard work, and toughness."

And it was the statue of Bill Mazeroski, the former Pittsburgh Pirates second baseman who hit the game-winning home run in the 1960 World Series. Stan said, "Inside Three Rivers Stadium there's a monument to the same thing." That was really nice.

Alzado was at the Pro Bowl working for ESPN. He was on the beach, and I walked by him. I wouldn't look at him. I had to walk right past him coming back and I kept my head down. Finally, I stopped, turned around, and said, "I'm sorry, I guess I haven't forgiven you for kicking my ass." He laughed and said, "Tunch, everybody gets their ass kicked by somebody. Just think maybe that ass kicking is what put you in the Pro Bowl this year." And he was right.

It was probably my most rewarding season for reasons that went beyond making the Pro Bowl. We had a real closeness on that team. In '88, as tough as it was, that year was special because we never quit despite going 5–11. We actually grew very close as a team instead of splintering due to all of the losses. A bunch of guys like Tim Johnson, Hardy Nickerson, Wolf, Keith Willis, Todd Blackledge, and I started getting together on Saturday nights and just praying. Not for wins or losses, just praying for each other and each other's families. The closeness on that team developed from the Murphy's Law of that year. We were 2–6 at the turn, and I said to Wolf, "This is a first. We've never been out of it by Halloween. Just think this is how the Tampa Buccaneers and certain teams always feel." But you played for pride, you played for integrity, you played for the guys next to you, and you played for yourself. I wanted to go through that year without giving up a sack and I think I only gave up one sack, maybe two.

We started 1989 like it was 1988 all over again. We lost 51–0 to the Cleveland Browns in the season opener at Three Rivers Stadium and then 41–10 the next week in Cincinnati. We were in a timeout in Cincinnati, and Mike Mularkey, who had signed with the Steelers as a free agent from the

Minnesota Vikings, looked at me and said, "This is the first time I've ever been part of anything this bad." Jokingly I said, "Stick with me, bro. You're going to go through a lot of firsts this year."

But Chuck stayed the course, and we got it together. We won our last three games, including the finale against the Buccaneers, to finish 9–7 but still needed a ton of help to make the playoffs. Sharon's sisters lived in Tampa, and I was just going to stay in Tampa because Sharon and the kids were there, and we were all together. But everything had fallen into place, and by the end of Sunday, we only needed Minnesota to beat Cincinnati the next night to make the playoffs.

I jumped on the plane and told Sharon, "I'll either be back here Tuesday, or you guys have a nice time without me." Cornerback Dwayne Woodruff had a bunch of guys at his house for the Vikings-Bengals game. It was a *Monday Night Football* game, and ABC had TV cameras at his home. Green Bay Packers linebacker Brian Noble had TV cameras at his house too because if Minnesota had lost, Green Bay would have gone to the playoffs. I was by myself and in bed watching the game. I had worked out that day and was still tired from our game the previous day. When it was late in the season, you didn't feel like doing anything so I was really, really tired. Wolf and I kept calling each other. Minnesota would go ahead, and I would say, "I'll pick you up in the morning." Cincinnati would jump ahead, and I'd say, "Okay, sleep in."

ABC was going back and forth between Woodruff's house and Noble's house during the game, and the Vikings ended up winning. Afterward, three cars outside of my house honked and people yelled, "Here we go, Steelers! Here we go!" It was just people who knew where I lived and drove past my house. I later told Mularkey, "See, I told you. A lot of firsts."

Our first opponent was the Houston Oilers, and I always hated to play in the Astrodome. One time we played in the Astrodome, and the air conditioning broke. It was hot, people were smoking back then, and the smoke just hung over the field. It was early in the season, and the baseball diamond was out since the Oilers shared the stadium with the Houston Astros. Wolf fell down on one of the bases, and it looked like he was covered with mud because he was sweating so bad. As we walked off the field at halftime, Chuck looked at Wolf and said, "Are we playing indoors or outdoors?"

I couldn't stand the Oilers during the Jerry Glanville era. There was a three-year stretch with Glanville where there were a lot of cheap shots and there was a lot of retaliation. We weren't afraid to take shots that would be considered cheap today. It was the way the game was played. Because they set the tone with cheap shots, we felt the liberty to retaliate. If I saw those guys in the street now, it would be great, like we were old friends.

The best way to explain that is when I was at the Pro Bowl with Mike Munchak, Bruce Matthews, and Ray Childress from those Oilers teams, all of the sudden, I realized they're good guys, and developing this animosity was just part of the game. Today players train together in the offseason and they get to be friendly, and there's free agency, so a lot of guys play on a lot of different teams. The players are more cordial to one another than it was in my day. When I played, you were on the field and you were battling, and there was just all of this animosity that built up. Then, when you were in a different environment with them, you realized, "Hey, these are pretty good guys," and probably guys thought that way about me. It is a fraternity, which makes the NFL such a special, special experience.

We had lost twice to Oilers in the regular season, and I just wanted to beat them so bad. Our third meeting was a very physical football game. It was fitting for the "House of Pain," which is what the Oilers and their fans called the Astrodome. Every play was so intense. I don't think they were overconfident, but they were cocky. When the game ended with us winning in overtime on a Gary Anderson field goal, I screamed at those guys, "House of Pain, baby! How does it feel?" That was one of my favorite wins as a Steeler.

We almost beat the Broncos the next week in Denver just as we had done in 1984. Merril Hoge had a great game, and Broncos safety Dennis Smith was miked and he kept saying, "We've got to stop Hoag! We've got to stop Hoag!" I kept yelling, "It's Hoge." He said, "Hoge, Hoag, whatever. We've got to stop him. We're making him look like Jim Brown."

We ran up and down the field on those guys. At one point, I came off the field and yelled, "These guys can't stop us!" The fans behind us were going crazy. Ron Blackledge said, "Settle down, would you? Just settle down."

Unfortunately for us, John Elway settled in and led the Broncos on one of his patented game-winning touchdown drives. I still can't believe we lost that game. We lost in the playoffs to great quarterbacks, and that position was the one thing that separated us from those teams after Terry retired in 1983.

Chuck retired quietly after the 1991 season, and I thought it was coming. Captains handed out gameballs, and after the Cleveland game at the end of '91, David Little, Bryan Hinkle, and I agreed we should give the gameball to Chuck. I said, "Coach, thanks for everything and a great season." He turned around and gave it to cornerback Ricky Shelton because he had two interceptions in that game, including a Pick-6.

We always visited my parents in San Francisco after the season ended, and I heard about Chuck's retirement out there. I called Steelers general manager Tom Donahoe from San Francisco and asked, "Who's going to be our new coach?" It was down to Bill Cowher and Dave Wannstedt. Bill got the job, and when I got back from San Francisco, I saw him and said, "Hey congratulations, Coach." He asked me into his office, and we talked about the team. A new era had begun.

Near Misses

Tunch Ilkin never made it to the Super Bowl in 13 seasons with the Steelers, and he and his teammates almost always had their playoffs end at the hands of a future Pro Football Hall of Fame quarterback. Here is the list of quarterbacks who defeated the Steelers in the postseason while Ilkin played for the Steelers:

Year	QB/Team	Score	Round
1982	Dan Fouts/Chargers	31–28	First Round of AFC Playoffs
1983	Jim Plunkett/Raiders	38–10	AFC Divisional Round
1984	Dan Marino/Dolphins	45–28	AFC Championship Game
1989	John Elway/Broncos	24–23	AFC Divisional Round
1992	*Frank Reich/Bills	24–3	AFC Divisional Round

*Reich filled in for the injured Jim Kelly in 1992 and engineered a comeback from a 35–3 deficit to beat the Houston Oilers 41–38 in the wild-card round of the AFC playoffs. He led the Buffalo Bills past the Steelers the following week at Three Rivers Stadium before turning quarterback duties over to Kelly, who had recovered from a knee injury.

CHAPTER 10

Turkish Temper

We had an intense week of practice prior to a 1983 playoff game against the Los Angeles Raiders in Los Angeles, and I went after Jack Lambert at one of them. Lambert had hit me from behind early in practice, and it was a cheap shot. I waited for an opportunity to get back at him, and it came near the end of practice. Craig Wolfley was blocking Lambert, and those two were about to get into it. I jumped over Wolf and started swinging at Lambert. It got broken up, and then Chuck Noll called practice over.

Calvin Sweeney, one of our wide receivers, started having some fun with it. "It's because you're Turkish," he said, "your Turkish temper." Then he started imitating me, saying, "I don't take any crap because I'm Turkish." He kept saying that over and over, just busting my chops.

It's funny because Tom Moore, our offensive coordinator, had told this story about serving with Turks during the Korean War. He told Wolf and me that the toughest, craziest guys were the Turks. He said, "Whenever we'd go into a town or a village, we'd ask them, 'What bar do you want?' And we'd take the other one because we didn't want to mess with them."

Anger was indeed part of my culture. My dad had a temper, my mom has a temper, and my uncles were tough guys. I played the game very hot-blooded and I always had kind of an inferiority complex. Early in my career, I couldn't take any crap because Rollie Dotsch, our offensive line coach, didn't want us to. He liked when you fought so I was trying to please him. I had felt the same way at Indiana State. I fought a lot and it was my own insecurity more than anything.

My first fight with the Steelers was against defensive lineman Tom Beasley, and it was when I came back after getting cut my rookie year. It was one of my first practices, and I was just trying to show that I belonged. He called me "Last Punch Tunch" because I always had to get the last punch in after a play. I got in my stance for one play, and he just unloaded on me. It was not simply jumping offside. He gave me a shot to the facemask and then

Our games against the Cleveland Browns during the 1980s and 1990s were always contentious and nasty. (Pittsburgh Steelers)

another one. I came up swinging, and we threw punches at one another. He yelled at me, "You better watch that last punch, Tunch!" We became really good friends after that, and he knew I was just trying to establish myself as a player.

My second year I got into a fight with defensive lineman Curtis Bunche. One of the newspaper headlines said something like, "We had a hunch Tunch would punch Bunche before lunch." Myron Cope went off with that. Another time I got into a fight with defensive tackle Tim Johnson, who is actually the nicest guy. He loves the Lord and he's a pastor at his own church. We started duking it out, and he yelled, "You don't have to win every pass rush! You don't have to win every battle!"

The thing is I felt like I *did* have to win every battle. I don't think I ever got over getting cut. Plus, I was relatively small, and that always lingered in the back of my mind. When we were playing the San Diego Chargers, I was in street clothes because of an injury. Chargers defensive tackle Burt Grossman looked at me and said, "Is that your normal weight?" I said, "Yeah." He said, "Man, I don't know why I was scared of you. You're not big at all."

It was really funny, and we had a good laugh about it. I was maybe 6'3" and 265 pounds, but I always wore my jersey so tight that my skinny arms actually looked big, and it made my legs look bigger than they were. I gave the illusion that I was bigger than I was.

There were no illusions about the nastiness that could take place when we played rivals such as AFC Central rivals like the Houston Oilers and Cleveland Browns. I actually loved playing in Cleveland Stadium. That place reeked of history. It reeked of urine, too, because the piping was all screwed up. The locker room was so small that you had to dress in shifts, and the drainage in the showers was terrible. If you showered late, there would be ankle-deep water in the shower. It was nasty. When you walked down the steps to the field, you had to duck or your head hit the lightbulbs. You marched down the steps and then you were in the dugout. You walked up three steps, and as soon as the Browns fans saw you, they started booing you and cussing you out. The Dawg Pound had started as a result of Frank Minnifield, Hanford Dixon, and Eddie Johnson. Those guys were always barking when they were on defense.

My rookie year we were warming up in the end zone near the Dawg Pound, and I was doing one-on-one drills with defensive end Dwight White. The fans were cussing him out. I thought, *Wow, they don't like us.* I started to take my helmet off after we had finished with our drills, and Dwight said, "Keep your helmet on, Holmes." No sooner had he said that, and a battery came flying across the field.

Another time we were in a timeout at Cleveland, and I got hit in the back of the head with a dog biscuit. I turned around and said, "Where did that come from? I'm going to go get that guy." Wolf laughed and said, "Relax. What are you going to do? This isn't *Slapshot?* You're not one of the Hanson brothers? You're going to find the guy that threw the dog bone at you? Just relax and let's get this ball in the end zone."

That's just the way Cleveland was. It was a nasty environment. We got in a fight there after I jumped on a guy who delivered a late hit. Someone then spiked the ball off my head, and Wolf went after him. We were all fighting, and the funny thing is Ray Snell, our starting left tackle, got kicked out of the game. And he wasn't anywhere near the play. When they started throwing the flags, someone yelled, "62 [my number] should be out of the game! 73 [Wolf's number] should be out of the game!" Wolf and I thought that one of us would be gone, but the head referee disqualified Snell, who yelled, "I didn't do anything! I didn't do anything!" The joke was I started it, Wolf finished it, and Snell got kicked out of the game for it.

In the 51–0 game that we lost to Cleveland in Three Rivers Stadium in 1989, Michael Dean Perry got into a fight with Chuck Lanza, one of our offensive linemen. He had Lanza by the facemask and he was drilling him. I saw it so I made a beeline and I was going to take out Perry. At the last minute, Perry saw me and he stopped. I went flying over the top and somersaulted over him. I swung at him and I missed, and the whole pile came down on me. I had my arms pinned to my sides, and guys were taking shots at me. The funny thing is I got fined for entering a fighting area and for fighting. Guys were saying, "You didn't even land a punch. You shouldn't be fined for fighting." It was almost like we were trying to get kicked out of that game, swinging at everybody.

I actually starred in scenes like that less and less as my career progressed. As I got older and grew in my faith, I learned how to control my temper. The problem with anger is it can be like an insatiable fire. What happens is you have the anger, you blow up, you get the release of these endorphins, and you feel good. You get the atta boy from your teammates because they're your brothers, and that feeds it. It wasn't until I started getting older that I realized I couldn't feed that monster, especially as a man who loves Christ. I needed to control that anger, and it's been a lifelong battle. I know how not to let it explode anymore, but it still wells up inside me. The Bible says, "Everything you do in word and deed, do as you do onto the Lord." I realized that I wanted to glorify God in my play.

It was a different game back then and it was a lot more fun. There was a lot of frontier justice in those days. If guys took a shot at your guy, you took a shot at them. There was an honor, I believe, in our game when I played. You played hurt. You played when you were sick.

I sound like an old curmudgeon when I say, "in my day," and Wolf and I laugh because we always say that on our radio show. But the game was different, and it was more intense. It challenged your manhood and it allowed you to test your own mettle. There was a real satisfaction to it. There was a satisfaction to going out there when you were sick and had a fever and were puking your guts out.

When we played at Denver in the 1989 playoffs, I had the flu and was going to the bathroom non-stop the night before the game. I had no idea how I was going to be able to play. I didn't eat anything at the pregame meal and took Lomotil, which is anti-diarrhea medicine. We got to the stadium, and I kept having to run to the bathroom. You can play if it is the flu and you are throwing up because you can throw up on the field. But you can't crap on the field. I took Lomotil every time I went to the bathroom. We went out for pregame warm-ups and after we came back to the locker room for final instructions, I went to the bathroom again and had to untape my hands. I took another Lomotil and thought, *This is bad. I'm going to be crapping my pants all game.* Well, it finally turned off, and I got to play the game. I was completely depleted, but I played the game, and we played pretty well. We should have won that game against the Broncos. That was Merril Hoge's big game with the 120 yards rushing, but we got Elwayed in the end. A funny postscript: I don't think I crapped for the next five days.

There were three games that I played—and I don't want this to sound like it is self-serving—where I was hurt or sick. One time we played *Monday Night Football* against the New York Jets and I had the flu and I was throwing up all night long. It was 1983, my first year as a starter, and I said I would just take it one play at a time until I couldn't go anymore. The only reason that I knew I should try to play sick was because both Mike Webster and Jon Kolb played sick. Those guys were the role models, they were the standard. So, you said, "Oh, Webby would have played, Kolby would have played, Larry Brown would have played. I'm going to play." I played that whole game and got through it so then I had a point of reference.

The next time I got sick we were playing in San Diego and I had a migraine headache and a sinus infection. My head felt like a beach ball that was about to burst. I took some medicine for it and finally fell asleep. The next day I played the whole game against the Chargers. Why? Because I had a point of reference. This isn't a pat on the back. We played sick. We played hurt.

Both of my rotator cuffs were partially torn for the final six games of the 1989 season and the two playoff games. They're still partially torn, and I had surgery on one of them on February 1, 2018. I took Novocain shots to kill the pain so I could play. I went to the Pro Bowl and played in the game before getting both shoulders cleaned out. Novocain always took the edge off, but it didn't take the pain completely away. You could torque your shoulders during the game because they were semi-numb. But on the plane ride home, the Novocain wore off, and I was in agony. Chuck always said on the first day of practice, "Take inventory of your body. This is the best you're going to feel all year."

The funny thing about the Novocain shots is that Doc Steele, or Paul Steele, was not the best with the needle. We were at Cleveland one time, and he was shooting Beas up before the game so Beas could play with a bad hamstring. Beas looked like he was trying to crawl up the wall. He had his hands on the wall, and Doc had that needle, which was about six inches long. He was trying to shove it up into that tendon, and the needle looked like it was bending. He finally shot all of the Novocain in there and pulled out the needle. Beas said, "You didn't get it, Doc." He had to do it again, and I looked at Beas and said, "Beas is a man."

The first time I got the needle we were playing the Bengals in Cincinnati. I had a badly bruised hand, and it felt broken. My hand went completely numb. There was a badge of honor playing hurt, and injuries were as much a part of the game as blocking and tackling.

The worst injury of my career happened during a Friday practice near the end of my career. It was 1990, and I was blocking defensive end Donald Evans while Barry Foster released on a route. Barry hit my arm hard enough that the back of my left hand went behind my left ear. My arm looked like a piece of spaghetti, and it was flopping as I fell to the ground. I was in pain and I said, "Oh, I'm not looking." Running back Warren Williams was the first to see it and he passed out. The trainers ran to Warren because he was out cold on the field. Guard Brian Blankenship stood over me and said, "Oh God! Somebody fix it! Put it back!" He tried to pick me up, and I said, "No, no, no! Leave me alone, man."

The trainers had to cut me out of my shoulder pads and they brought out an equipment crate and carried me into the locker room. They immobilized my dislocated elbow, and linebacker Bryan Hinkle started messing with me. Hink always called me "Happy Guy" because I was always smiling. He said, "What's up, Happy Guy? Not so happy now." He was making me laugh, and I said, "Don't make me laugh. Every time I laugh it vibrates." Hink said, "Don't watch that on film." I said, "Why not?" He said, "Because if you watch it on film, you'll retire."

They put me in an ambulance and took me to Divine Providence Hospital. On the way there, we hit this big pothole, and pain just shot up my arm. I thought, *Oh man, what's it going to feel like when they reduce it? If it hurt that much coming out, what's it going to feel like when they pop it back in?* They took an X-ray of it, and the doctor said, "Oh, it's back in." I said, "Oh, it must have been the pothole." That was the first time I thanked God for potholes.

There was no Vicodin in our day, and the strongest drugs we took were Tylenol and codeine. Ralph Berlin, our longtime trainer, never gave them unless you showed you were really injured. I would say, "Ralph, my shoulder's been killing." He would say, "Here's some Tylenol." I would say,

"Ralph, my pain laughs at Tylenol." But the Steelers were very conscious of that. They never gave out drugs.

Concussions and the handling of them are a hot-button issue right now. I had two of them with the Steelers, and both times I was pulled from the game. The first time was my rookie year on a kickoff. I ran into a wedge, and all of the sudden the colors in Buffalo's Rich Stadium got very bright. I felt like I was stoned.

The second time happened as Bengals safety David Fulcher returned an interception for a touchdown. I tackled him at the goal line, and his knee hit me in the side of the head. I tried to shake it off because I had gotten dinged before and been able to shake it off and clear the cobwebs so to speak. The next series I cut my guy three plays in a row and I never cut my guy. I hated cutting guys because I had no confidence in my cutting ability. I did three times in a row because I was off-balance. I came off the field, and Noll said, "What is wrong with you?" I said, "I'm a little blurry." I saw Dr. Joseph Maroon and said, "If I close one eye, I can see perfect." He said, "I don't care if you can see out of one eye. The fact that you've got to close one eye to see is what I'm worried about. You're not going back out there." He told them to take my helmet because I was going to try to run out there after my second concussion. It was absolute bullcrap the heat Maroon took in the movie *Concussion*. Doc Maroon, who is still with the Steelers, cares for the players and is a great doctor.

As Doc Maroon said, the brain is a muscle, and, like any other muscle, I think it works on a use-it-or-lose-it principle. I'm always memorizing rosters and scripture verses. I use my brain more now than when I was in college. Are there guys who have post-concussion syndrome or CTE? Yes, but it's almost like there is a movement to vilify football, like *Oh my gosh, it's so barbaric.* I feel horrible for the guys who have problems, and if a guy is messed up and he's dealing with severe dementia, that guy should be taken care of. I understand the concussion issue and I understand with the lawsuits that you have to crack down on hits to the head. But when you sign up to play this game, it's not like, *Oh gee, something could happen to me?* You signed up for it.

I would have liked to have gotten paid what the players get paid today, but I am happy I played in the era that I did. And my problem with the NFL in general is that they are constantly tweaking. They are always changing the rules. They never leave well enough alone. Every year there's something different. There's probably been more than 200 rules changes just since I retired after the 1993 season, and it's ridiculous.

They're trying to make the game more civilized, and I think the league oversteers the car. If something happens one way, they try to change everything to make it not happen again. The game is rough, physical, and nasty. As Chuck used to say, it's not for the faint of heart. I'll be honest: I'm not sure I could play today. You can't go to the head, you can't go to the face. The NFL really limits you in the physicality of the game, and you've got to be physical. Today you throw a guy on the ground, and they immediately flag you. It's not holding if a guy is off-balance and you throw him to the ground and then you gore him when he's on the ground. You're trying to finish him. To quote Chuck again, you're trying to impose your will on the will of your opponent. It's part of the game. It's football; it's not going to be safe. Football is not for everybody, and, as Chuck always said, if it was easy, everybody would do it.

CHAPTER 11

Offensive Line: A Band of Brothers

Craig Wolfley has always had my back. I found that out early in our Steelers' careers down in Houston. We were playing the Oilers in the final game of the 1981 season and were down to one quarterback, Mark Malone, because of injuries to Terry Bradshaw and Cliff Stoudt.

I was on the field for short-yardage and goal-line situations by the end of my first full NFL season, and Malone had scored a touchdown on a quarterback run. Oilers safety Vernon Perry speared Malone a good five seconds after he had scored. Malone was on his knees, and I was trailing the play. I brought a punch from the top of my socks and tagged Perry in the end zone. Oilers linebacker Ted Washington jumped on me, and Wolf jumped on him. We were in the end zone, just punching and screaming.

Perry said, "Sixty-two, I'm going to meet you after the game and I'm gonna kill you." I went crazy and started yelling, "Bring it on! Bring it on!" Wolf and I were standing on the sideline near the end of the game, and I said, "Wolf, watch my back. I'm going after Vernon Perry." I started running across the field after the final whistle, and because of the fights, there wasn't a whole lot of shaking hands. Perry took off and went to the locker room. I was looking for the guy who threatened to kill me, and we were on the Oilers sidelines, essentially in no-man's land.

Wolf's Words

 After Ted Washington jumped on Tunch's back, I went after him, and we slugged it out a little bit. Once everything got broken up, the crowd parted, and there was Washington and there was me, and we started all over again. It was crazy, and they just threw offsetting flags and separated us to the sidelines. That's when Tunch said, "Watch my back. Because when the gun goes off, I'm going to go get Perry." About halfway over I realized it was Tunch and me headed to the Houston sidelines and nobody in reserve. I thought, *I wonder if this is a good idea*. When he got that wild-eyed Turkish look, I knew that he might do something stupid, but buddies have each other's backs.

Wolf and I played 10 seasons together with the Steelers and we are now part of the Steelers' radio broadcast team. We also do a daily radio show together during the season as well as Steelers TV shows. We literally see each other every day during the football season, and it has been that way most of our lives here in Pittsburgh. His mom says I am like a son to her; my mom says he is like a son to her. I had the privilege of baptizing Wolf's son, Kyle, before he left for Afghanistan, and Megan, his daughter. What a blessing to be able to do that.

The first time I met Wolf was at Steelers rookie orientation in 1980, the weekend right after the draft. I got picked up first, and Wolf came off a different plane right after me. I looked at him and thought, *Damn, he's big.* My rookie year in training camp, I roomed with Billy Hurley, and he and Wolf had played together at Syracuse. We all hung out together, and Wolf and I got to be buddies pretty quick.

We went to Burger King our first year together, and he said, "I want two Double Whoppers, large fries, and a Diet Coke." I said, "Diet Coke?" He said, "I've gotta save them where I can." Regarding Wolf's feats of eating, even people today say, "Are those exaggerations?" I say, "No, fact is stranger than fiction."

The offensive linemen had what we called a spike fund during the season, and if you got called for a penalty, it was a buck a yard. If you gave up a sack,

The offensive line is a close-knit group, and because of that, Craig Wolfley always had my back. (Pittsburgh Steelers)

it was $20. If you made a mental error, it was $20. If we rushed for 150 yards or if we didn't give up any sacks, Ron Blackledge, our position coach, put in $20. We would have a couple of $1,000 in the kitty by the end of the season and would go somewhere nice for dinner.

One time we went to this place called Hugo's Rotisserie, and Wolf ate three whole roasted ducks, two racks of lamb, two shrimp cocktails, one escargot, French onion soup, salad, and dessert. That was when Ted Petersen gave him the "Mindless Eating Machine" nickname.

I could tell Wolf and offensive line stories all day.

We always considered ourselves a bunch of guys who cared for one another. When we were playing the Cleveland Browns, they came with this blitz and they sandwiched Mark. His helmet popped off, and he was literally unconscious. Not only was his helmet off, but his ear pads were out, and there was blood on his mouth. Wolf, Mike Webster, and I all grabbed the guys we were blocking and said, "I've got my guy!" So much for caring for our fallen teammate and buddy Mark. We were more concerned about not getting blamed for the sack.

When we were playing the Los Angeles Rams, they were running a twist to our side, and I was playing on the left side next to Wolf. I stumbled coming out of my stance, and Reggie Doss, the defensive end on my side, took one step up the field and just earholed Wolf. We got back to the huddle, and he said, "Do you think you could just take a *little* off of him? Just a little bit off of him!" I was laughing because I knew I screwed up by not protecting his hip and I knew he was mad. He said, "Oh yeah, it's pretty funny. What if I go ahead and do the same thing?" I said, "I'm sorry. I'm just kidding, I'm just kidding." We argued in the huddle, and he finally said, "Make sure you protect my hip!" I said, "All right, buddy. I've got your hip."

But Wolf blew me up pretty good one time and didn't even own up to it. We were playing the Los Angeles Raiders at the Coliseum in the last game of the 1984 season and we had to beat them to get into the playoffs. I was playing right tackle, and if Howie Long came upfield, I had to block him. If Long went inside, I had to go up on Matt Millen, the linebacker. I was pass protecting, and Long rammed inside and I slammed into Millen. All of the sudden, I got drilled in the tailbone. It was Wolf, and he realized that he had blocked the wrong guy. He jumped up and got back to the huddle, and I was still on the ground. When I finally got back to the huddle, I said, "Someone cheap-shotted me!" Wolf said, "Uh, did you get a number?" I said, "No, I don't know who did it."

I sat on ice the whole four-hour flight home from Los Angeles. We got to treatment the next day, and I had to sit on ice again. We watched film on Tuesday, the play came up, and I saw who the culprit was. I said to Wolf, "You turd, it was you all along," He and Webby were cracking up, just laughing so hard. He will tell you he made a very athletic move, but he made a mental mistake.

Wolf's Words

 At the snap of the ball, Cliff Stoudt turned and faked a pitch wide to the back. Howie Long took one step to the inside and then he turned and ran to the outside. Tunch saw Long take the one step inside and he went up to the second level to get Millen. I pulled from left guard, but if I hit Long, I was hitting somebody who had taken himself out of the play. I make a great athletic adjustment with cat-like stealth and quickness and turned up on Millen. I had the horns down, and the flaps were lowered and I was ready for contact. Sixty-two flashed right in front of

my eyes, but I didn't have airbrakes so I couldn't pull off. Tunch hit Millen two heartbeats before I did. I was already in launch mode, and we all went down in a heap. Tunch was down on the ground holding his lower back area and he was in real pain. I just went back to the huddle. I was in the huddle, and Stoudt said, "We're down a guy." I said, "Who could that be?" And I knew darn well what had just happened.

Eight seconds later Tunch came back into the huddle dragging his leg. I said, "Tunch, what happened? Did you get a look at the number who hit you?" He sucked it up and he played. We got on the plane after the game and he was in agony. We flew all the way from L.A. to Pittsburgh and he said, "I can't believe somebody hit me in the ass like that." I said, "Wow, I can't either." The next day was an off day. It was a darned thing if you had to go to the stadium for treatment because that would've been your only day being away from the stadium and away from football. Tunch had to go in for treatment while I was at home living large on the couch with my remote control. I totally forgot about the hit until we went to meetings on Tuesday. It just didn't occur to me the play was going to come up and be shown in graphic detail. They showed the play in regular speed. They showed it in slow motion. They showed it forward. They showed it backward. Tunch looked over and just eviscerated me. We call it the "friendly fire case." Never admit anything unless they show the film.

I got to laugh at Wolf's pain on a plane ride home a different time. He had broken his thumb and he was saying all week, "How am I going to play with this?" We had a saying, "The needle is your friend. Let's go to the block party." It was called that because the Novocain shot blocked the pain. Back in our day, guys took the needle all of the time. Nobody ever made you take the needle; you took it voluntarily. And I will say this:

playing hurt was a badge of honor. L.C. Greenwood always said, "Anybody can play this game healthy."

Wolf practiced all week one-handed, but after he got his shot, he said, "Look at this?" He was banging his thumb on his helmet, saying, "Isn't this great! I wonder if you can get this in your whole body." He was just hammering the helmet and he played and made it through the game. On the way home, the Novocain wore off, and all of the sudden he went, "Aaaah! This is killing me!"

Wolf was a heck of a player. If he hadn't torn up his knee, he would have gone to multiple Pro Bowls. He was strong, athletic, and started as a second-year guy. The first time I watched him in one-on-one drills against defensive tackle Steve Furness, he "wired" him—or punched him, stopping him dead in his tracks—and then he got in a fight. I looked at Wolf and said, "Wow, he's good." Wolf got unlucky with injuries, but he had the strength to brawl with you and he had the hand quickness to punch you.

He was fast, too, and we used to compete to see who was faster. My second or third year, we ran the 40-yard dash. He went first and then said, "4.89, brother. Beat that." I tried to beat it and pulled my hamstring. He was cracking up and he said, "Oh, you pulled your hammy trying to beat me in the 40? That will teach you. I'm faster."

Wolf had a series of injuries one training camp and almost reached the breaking point.

I was going to the cafeteria, and he passed me and said, "I'm done. I'm retiring. I can't take it anymore. My shoulder hurts, my groin's gone, it feels like I've got glass in my knee." I said, "Wait a second." The dining room was about to close, and I didn't want to miss dinner. I said, "Look, do me a favor. Go back to the room and don't do anything until I come back. Promise me?" He said, "All right." I said, "Don't go talk to Chuck, don't do anything. Wait there for me."

I ate and hustled back to the room. He said, "I'm telling you, I can't do this anymore." I said, "Wait a second, stop. What are you going to do for a living?" He said, "I don't know. Maybe I'll work for Allied Van Lines." I said, "So you're going to move furniture? That's a very honorable profession but…is that what you're going to do? Don't be an idiot. You don't even have your degree. Relax, this too shall pass." He looked at me and said, "Yeah, you're right." That put a stop to that.

That was probably in our fifth year with the Steelers. The closeness between Wolf and I reflected my friendship with my fellow offensive linemen in general. Offensive linemen are unique because we do more together than probably any other position group. We hunt together, we fish together, we eat together. We're cut from the same cloth, and offensive linemen are wound tighter than everybody else because the only time anyone calls your name is if you get called for holding or if you give up a sack.

I don't know what genius decided to mike referees. But if you heard, "holding, No. 62," someone the next day said, "Hey, Tunch, saw you got called for holding and got that touchdown called back, tough break for you buddy." As a result of that, we really lock arms and bind closer together than every other position. We always said, "Protect the franchise. I don't care if you have to kick, bite, scratch, hold. Don't let anybody get to the quarterback." In the huddle we said, "All right guys, it's nut cutting time. Don't let anybody near our guy."

We had some fun with that ethos one time. We were playing the New York Giants in the final regular-season game of 1985, and they were on the fringe of breaking the NFL season sack record. They had all of these great players like Lawrence Taylor, Leonard Marshall, Jimmy Burt, Harry Carson, George Martin, and Carl Banks. We were sitting at the pregame meal, and it was Ray Pinney, Wolf, Webby, Mark, and me. Ray said, "I kind of feel like I'm playing against the Pro Bowl on my side." Webby said, "We're all playing in the Pro Bowl. Every one of these guys is a Pro Bowler." Mark said, "Well, we have to get after them." Webby said, "We can't block these guys. Leonard Marshall! L.T.! Jimmy Burt! George Martin! Carl Banks! There's no way we can block these guys." I looked at Malone, and he was getting paler and paler. I said, "He's just joking, Mark." Webby said, "No, I'm not! There's no way we can block these guys! My advice to you? One-thousand one…one-thousand two get rid of the ball." It was really funny because they needed four sacks in that game to break the record but didn't get it.

Webby was always the voice of gloom and doom. Any freak thing that happened, he told us about it, usually on Saturday before we got on a flight. He told us this story about a circus performer who was launched the wrong way, and a hippo swallowed him and killed him. There was a rock slide one time on Route 51, and every time he was driving on 51 after that, he went way to the left or way to the right because he thought the rock slide would come at him. He also vowed never to go to the Indianapolis 500 because of the guy who got killed when a tire got launched way up into the stands after a wreck.

Webby was paranoid. When he crossed the picket line in 1987, he called me in tears since I was the Steelers' player representative. He said, "They're going to cut me." I said, "Webby, they're not going to cut you," but he really believed they would if he didn't cross the picket line. That's why he was so driven, I guess, because he was always so paranoid.

He was also the hardest working guy I ever saw. One year Webby came back from the Pro Bowl and went straight to Three Rivers Stadium to run steps. I said, "Who does that?" He was just as obsessive with his preparation, knowing what the defense was doing, knowing what everybody did on offense.

If a meeting in the weight room was at 9:00 and you walked in at 8:00, Webby and Jon Kolb had already been there for an hour, sweating. I left early after practice once and stuck my head in the offensive line weight room. I saw Webby, Kolby, and Larry Brown and said, "Okay, that's what you do." Webby never missed a play. Since I was the backup center early in my career, I never played a snap at center except for the preseason. One game Webby was out on a screen pass and he ducked his head. I thought he broke his neck, but he got up and stumbled back to the huddle. He said in this high voice, "I think I broke my f----- neck. I think I broke my f----- neck." I went running out there, and said, "Webby, I've got you." He said, "Get the hell out of here." It was crazy.

My rookie year he tore the cartilage in his knee against the Kansas City Chiefs, and we were playing in Houston that Thursday night. He was on crutches until pregame. He went out for drills and said, "I can't do this." They cut his tape off, and he said, "Try taping it this way." They re-taped it, and he went out and played the whole game. He played the last game of the season too, played in the Pro Bowl, *and then* got surgery.

Webby was not only weight room strong but country strong. He would get those clamps on you and once he had you under the armpits it was over. Webby was the celebrity spokesman for spina bifida and he would hold these little spina bifida babies in his hands, and it was such a contrast. Here was this loving side of this guy who was so good that the guys playing against him would quit.

He had such an impact on both Wolf and me and was just a wonderful, wonderful man. He always made you think you could play and he always invited me to work out with him and watch extra film with him. Webby was in great shape and he won every 350-yard run. He set the standard, and we tried to keep up with him because we ran five 350-yarders after every practice. Wolf said, "I'm gonna get him." Wolf was running stride for stride with Webby, and I was right behind trying to catch up. We finished, and Wolf collapsed. He was on the ground, and I thought Webby was saying something nice to him. But apparently, Webby said, "Wolf, if it comes down to you dying or my giving you mouth-to-mouth, consider yourself a dead man."

Webby had a great sense of humor and he loved quoting John Wayne movies. After one bad loss, we were going to watch film and we knew it was going to be bad. Webby said, "Okay, let's get to the rat killing." That was a line out of *True Grit*. Another time we were stretching, and Webby said, "Don't say it's a fine morning, or I'll shoot ya!" That was a line from *McClintock!* He always quoted whatever John Wayne movie we were watching at the time.

We played the Chiefs in 1989, and it was the year that Webby had gone to Kansas City.

There is a picture of Webby, Wolf, and me from after that game. Webby is in his Kansas City white, and Wolf and I are in our Steelers black and we've got our arms around each other. It's one of my favorite pictures, but it was also really sad because Webby wasn't with us anymore.

Webby was my hero. He had such tenacity and those hands—he just grabbed you and buckled you. Doug Marrone, the head coach of the Jacksonville Jaguars, and I used to argue over who was better: Miami Dolphins center Dwight Stephenson or Webby. Stephenson had the athleticism and speed, and Webby had the tenacity, physicality, and strength. Put them together and you've got Dermontti Dawson, who succeeded Webby at center for the Steelers. Dirt Dawson was never as tenacious as Webby, but man, was he strong.

Late in September of 1989, I walked into the weight room, and Dirt said, "Tunch, do you want to work out?" I said, "Sure." We went to the bench press, and I was doing 315 pounds. He put 405 pounds on and just banged it out. He said, "I don't want to do too much today." I said, "Why not?" He said, "I haven't lifted in a while and I don't want to get sore." I said, "When was the last time that you lifted?" He said, "Oh, well before camp." I said, *"Before camp?"*

Dirt could strike what is called a rising blow. He had that quick twitch. Webby was more of a plodder; Dirt was just explosive. Webby was more straight ahead. But they both got the job done.

Dirt was the first center that I ever saw pull, and he got out and just crushed guys. The thing about Dirt, too, is he was just so carefree. Pressure never got to him. Most offensive linemen are really nervous because they don't want to give up a sack or get called for holding. They're just wound tight. Dirt once got a penalty on a play that was very influential on the outcome of the game. In the locker room after the game, I put my arm around him and said, "Don't worry about it." He said, "Oh yeah, Tunch, I'm not worried about it. I forgot about it already." I just thought, *I wish I was like that.*

There is one notable time when Dirt wasn't his normal relaxed self, and it is a pretty funny story. We were playing the Chiefs on *Monday Night Football*, and they ran this 4-4 defense. On the surface you didn't know where the strength was, so the center had to identify the MIKE linebacker and call the blocking scheme. Dirt was a spokesman for UPTIME, an energy pill, and he took a couple of them before the game. It was the first time he had ever taken them. His heart started racing, and his brains were going from here to there. We were sitting on the bench, and he said, "Tunch, you've got to make the calls! I'm freaking out! I'm freaking out!" The coaches looked at him like, *Is he okay?* I said, "It's going to be okay. I've got it. I'll make the calls." It was hilarious. He never took another UPTIME.

Another great lineman I played with was Larry "Bubba" Brown, who played tight end and actually caught a touchdown pass in the Steelers' first Super Bowl before moving to right tackle. His arms were bigger than his waist, and he had these triceps that were like coconuts. The joke was Bubba would walk into a room, and his triceps would come in about 30 seconds later. When he punched you, he sent you flying and he played very compact for a 6'4" guy who weighed 275 pounds. He was just great, and I can't believe he only went to one Pro Bowl. Bubba was another one who would just make guys quit.

Bob Kohrs tells the story of when Bubba made Mark Gastineau cry during the time of the New York Sack Exchange. He didn't literally make him cry but, according to Kohrs, Gastineau was teary eyed after the game because Bubba just continually destroyed him. He was a great player and a great guy. Chuck Noll said Bubba should be in the Hall of Fame, and I agree. I'm a huge fan of his.

If there was a Hall of Fame for characters, Steve Courson might be a charter member.

He was the nicest guy, but people were scared of him. We went to visit Gary Dunn in Florida and went fishing in the Keys. We walked through this tiki bar/restaurant, and Courson, who was 300 pounds and just shredded, had a camouflage tank top on, a camouflage headband, and aviator sunglasses. As he walked, the ground shook, and moms grabbed their kids. I would stop by his house in the middle of the day and he would be watching *The World at War* and talking about the Battle of Stalingrad. He knew every battle from Gettysburg to World War II. He was a history nut and could just recite stuff.

He was so smart but sometimes lacked common sense. Chuck once sent him in with a play, but he didn't say anything to Terry, who thought he was just coming in as a substitute, not as messenger. Terry started calling *Blue 33 Trap. Blue 33 Trap.* Steve looked at him and said, "No, that ain't it. That ain't the play." Terry said, "You didn't tell me the play! Timeout!"

Steve was a tremendous athlete and at 6'1", 285 pounds could run a high 4.6, low 4.7 time in the 40-yard dash. His strength and speed made him scary good at times as Cincinnati Bengals linebacker Reggie Williams once found out. Steve led a sweep on one play and he put the horns on Williams, who tried to swim over the block but got caught up in the air. Steve did not break his stride, and the first thing that hit the ground was the heels of Williams' feet. The next thing that hit was the back of his head. Steve just ran right through him, stomped on him, and picked up the safety without altering his stride. It was the best block I've ever seen in my life.

By his own admission, Steve was a steroid, alcohol, and drug abuser. He got really sick and almost died of cardiomyopathy. He quit drinking, quit doing drugs. He gave his life to Christ. He really changed, and his heart rejuvenated. He started on a light exercise program—he wasn't trying to bench press 600 pounds anymore—and he started riding a bike really lightly, not getting his heart into oxygen debt and got better.

Steve died tragically at the age of 50 in 2005 when he was chopping down a tree. He was afraid it was going to fall on his dog, Rachel, and he tried to grab her and the tree fell on him. He is one of a number of Steelers from the 1970s and 1980s who died young, and some of them were really close friends of mine. Webby's struggles before he passed in 2002 are well-documented, and the death of two other offensive linemen really hit me hard as well.

Tyrone McGriff was in my draft class and he was actually the first of the offensive linemen of that class to start, even though he was taken with the last overall pick in 1980. Tyronne couldn't have been more than 6'0" and was probably 270 pounds, but he was so athletic. He had a knack for adjusting better in space than anyone and he was so low to the ground that you couldn't run him over. Louie Kelcher, a San Diego Chargers defensive tackle who made three Pro Bowls, once asked Webby, "Who's 61? I tried to bull rush him and I thought he was standing on a barrel. I thought this guy was going to be a piece of meat for me, and that guy is good."

Tyronne was also the most jovial guy, always smiling, a fun guy in the locker room. I saw him in 2000 at a football clinic when he was coaching at Florida A&M and I was speaking there. It was down in Orlando, and I heard, "Tunch!" We hugged and said, "How come we don't get together? We should get together." That was in May, and he died the following Thanksgiving from a massive heart attack.

Terry Long took his own life in 2005, and he and I played next to one another on the offensive line after I moved exclusively to right tackle in 1985. We were close friends, and he was so strong and funny. When we played the Cardinals in Arizona in 1988, it was like 120 degrees and we were behind and throwing the ball on every play. Long was grabbing onto me, saying, "I can't do it anymore. I can't do it anymore. Put the kid in." I said, "Would you quit grabbing me? I'm tired too!"

Another time he and I were getting treatment, and Long walked past us. I said, "Chuck, how you doing?" It took almost to the end of my career before I could call our legendary coach "Chuck." It was always "Coach Noll" before I got comfortable calling him Chuck. It sounded like I had called him Chuckie, but I didn't, and Long said, "Chuckie? How could you call him Chuckie?" Chuck was standing right there and he said, "A rose by any other name is still a rose." Then he walked out.

Terry and I had the kind of friendship where we could bust each other's chops, but he also had severe mood swings. Sometimes you would ask him, "How are you doing?" And he would say, "What are you doing, writing a book?" It would be like, *Okay, you're like that today.* Terry had tried to take his life with rat poison while he was playing. He tested positive for steroids and sunk into a deep depression. You always worried about him because he isolated himself.

One night he called me and said, "Tunch, I just want to thank you for being my friend. I love you and good-bye." He then hung up. I called him back, and he wouldn't pick up. I called Dermontti and told him what happened. I said, "Dirt, I think he's going to do something crazy." So Dirt and I met up and went to Terry's house. We pounded on the door, and he didn't answer. We did it again, and he didn't answer. Finally, Terry came to the door and said, "Hey, what's up guys?" like nothing had happened. I said, "You don't call someone up and say thank you for being my friend, I love you, good-bye. You don't do that." He said, "I just wanted to tell you that I appreciate you." We went in and had a couple of beers and threw darts all night.

I talked to him right before he took his life in 2005. He said, "Tunch, I'm just not made for this world. I want to go be with the Lord." I said, "Terry, the Lord may not be done with you yet. He may have other things for you." He said, "I know I'm saved because I love Him and I know He died on the cross for me. I'm not meant for this world." I said, "Just relax. Let's you and me and Wolf go out to lunch this week. How about Thursday?" He said, "Thursday's a good day." It was either late Monday night or early Tuesday morning when he took his life and it was just so devastating.

Losing so many former teammates and close friends probably makes my bond with Wolf that much stronger. As close as we are, we have gotten into arguments, including a memorable one in 1988. We really struggled as a team that season and went 5–11. We were in the airport walking to our gate for an away game, and Wolf said, "Look at you. You look awful preppy today." I looked at him, and he was kind of disheveled, and his clothes were wrinkled, so I said, "Well, at least I don't look like yesterday's newspaper." We started yelling at each other in the airport. We were chin to chin almost like we're ready to duke. Some lady said to her husband, "No wonder they're losing. They're fighting amongst each other." He went one way, and I went one way. We met 15 minutes later and apologized. We really did have each other's back and we always will.

CHAPTER 12

The Strike and
Mr. Rooney's Honor

Everything I've learned about leadership I've learned through the Steelers organization. I saw things that I admired in Art Rooney and Dan Rooney. I saw humility, and that's the way I wanted to be. In Mike Webster and Jon Kolb, I saw mentorship. I also saw that in Donnie Shell, John Stallworth, and Joe Greene. I saw those leadership traits in men that I wanted to emulate.

The first strike happened in 1982 when I was still finding my way with the Steelers. That came at a really inopportune time for me both on the field and away from it. We opened the 1982 season with wins against the Dallas Cowboys and Cincinnati Bengals and were playing really good football. Larry Brown got hurt, and I played right tackle in relief of him during the second half of the Cincinnati game. I thought, *Wow, I'm playing.*

We went on strike after that, and the only good thing about it was it allowed my ankle to heal. I had sprained it against the Bengals, and the trainers had taped it up really tight so I was able to play the rest of the game.

When they took the tape off after the game, my ankle exploded. It swelled up so bad that it looked like I had elephantiasis.

During the strike we worked out in Pitt's weight room and practiced at Pitt Stadium. Pitt was very gracious to us, and that was when I first met Jim Sweeney, who later played for the Steelers. We were working out, and he said, "Tunch, I was recruited by Indiana State." I jokingly asked, "Well, why would you pick Pitt over Indiana State?" We both had a good laugh at that.

The scary thing was that as the strike dragged on it looked like the whole season might get cancelled. Sharon and I were newlyweds, and I was thinking, *I've got to make a living*. A neighbor of mine sold insurance, and I went to an insurance seminar, thinking if we didn't settle the labor dispute, I would sell insurance. It was in a hotel and after listening to the presentation

A teammate listens to me (in the vest) and Craig Wolfley (far right) as we picket outside Three Rivers Stadium during the strike of 1987.

I said, "Oh man, I don't know if I can do this. I'm not a salesman." All of this stuff was going through my brain on the drive home, but I said to myself, *Well, you've got to do what you've got to do.* I walked in the door, and Sharon said, "The strike is over. You're going back to work tomorrow." I was so excited.

That was the year we called the playoffs the Super Bowl tournament because a lot of teams got into the playoffs since the season had been shortened to nine games. We played the San Diego Chargers in the opening round of the playoffs at Three Rivers Stadium and we led late in the game. I thought, *We're going to the Super Bowl,* but Dan Fouts brought the Chargers back. On the final drive of the game, he rolled to the right and threw a screen pass to the left to Kellen Winslow. He scored a touchdown, and the season was over just like that.

Labor peace didn't last long, and by the time another strike loomed in the late 1980s, I found myself in an unenviable position. Bobby Kohrs had been our player rep, and I had been helping him out. I was the assistant player rep, but I didn't want to be the player rep after Bobby left the Steelers following the 1985 season.

I went into our first meeting after Bobby had left, and someone said, "Hey, since Kohrs is gone we need a new player rep." Webby said, "Tunch, you should be the player rep," and everybody jumped on that. I said no but to no avail. The next thing you know, I'm the player rep, and we're getting ready for a strike, which was a big challenge. My teammates may have been more than happy to make me Bobby's replacement, but they were not as eager to help me with those duties. I said, "Who wants to be assistant player rep?" Not one hand went up. I said, "C'mon, someone's got to be the assistant player rep." Not one hand. We left the meeting, and I don't know if I asked Craig Wolfley or if he offered, but we got to a point in the conversation where he said, "Look, if no one will be the assistant player rep, I'm not going to leave you hanging out there." He became the assistant player rep because he felt sorry for me.

As the Steelers' player representative, I headed a group that went to Los Angeles in 1987 to try to avert a strike. I picked the leadership team, and nobody really wanted to be on it. It included Bubby Brister, Gary Dunn, and, of course, Wolf. I told Bubby, "Now listen, this isn't a party trip. I expect you to go to these meetings." The morning of the first meeting, he wasn't there. He had been out a little bit too late. I called him, and he didn't answer. I gave the maid $20 to give me a key to his room. It was pitch dark when I went into Bubby's room. I opened up the windows and ripped his blankets off him. He yelled, "Tunch!" I yelled back, "Get up and go to the meeting! I brought you here for the meetings, not to be an idiot!"

During the night we went on strike, we had a secret meeting at Froggy's in Pittsburgh. We showed up at Froggy's, and everybody with a media badge in Pittsburgh was there. I said, "How did you guys find out about it? This is a secret meeting." I used to ask longtime Steelers beat writer Ed Bouchette, "How did you know everything we were going to do before we did it? Who was leaking it?" He still won't tell me. While we were on strike, we agreed there should only be one voice coming out of our locker room, and it was mine. Those guys loved me for it because they didn't have to answer controversial questions.

Wolf and I ran into some controversy when we met with the Allegheny Labor Council while the Steelers were practicing in Johnstown, Pennsylvania, with a mixture of replacement players and ones who had crossed the picket line. It didn't take long for the meeting to get contentious, and some of their guys were saying, "How can you ask us to honor the strike?" I said, "Whoa, whoa, wait a second. I haven't asked anybody to honor our strike. You asked for the meeting. Here we are." One guy said, "I'm not going to line up with the Steelers. These guys make their big money, and the first thing they do is they buy foreign cars made with foreign steel." I said, "Wait a second, wait a second. I've got a Suburban."

Then Wolf got up and said, "Let me tell you something. I've got parts of me scattered from here to San Francisco. Don't tell me what kind of car I can buy and what kind I can't."

I grabbed Wolf and said, "Just relax." Then the head of the iron workers union from Johnstown looked straight at me and said, "All I know is I've got 50 scabs in Johnstown and I don't see you doing anything about it. How come you guys are down here?"

I snapped after telling Wolf to settle down. I said, "Don't tell me how to run my strike. I run my strike the way I want to run my strike. We'll be up there picketing when we're damn well ready to." Wolf grabbed me and said, "You need to take your own advice." The strike was such an education right away. I found out what we do as a labor union affects other labor unions. We left the meeting and we left in—of all cars—Wolf's Mercedes. I said, "We should have drove my Suburban," and he said, "Yeah, I'm sorry."

Later I got a call from Bill Parise, who was the executive director of the Pittsburgh YMCA. Bill, who later became James Harrison's agent, is an old buddy of mine and he said, "Tunch, you guys can use our weight room and our conference room and our offices." That became our headquarters. That was where we were lifting when I got a call from Dan Rooney. He said, "I hear you're looking for a field." I said, "I am." He said, "Go into my office. There's a key on Mary Ann's desk to the practice field. You didn't get it from me."

We practiced every day on the grass field thanks to the ambassador, and it shouldn't have come as a surprise. Before we went on strike, he said, "Keep them together, Tunch. Keep them together." That was his mandate. We always talked, and one time he said to me, "Look we've got crazies on both sides. I've got crazies on my side, and you've got crazies on your side." He always said, "We've got to do what's good for the game," and that's why he got along so well with former NFL Players Association executive director Gene Upshaw because Upshaw felt the same way.

My job was to understand everything that was going on, and eventually I felt like I had earned a minor in antitrust law. My prayer was that I would not allow my bias to enter into how I felt about the union leadership as well as not to go back to the union leadership and falsely represent my team. I was hung up on doing everything by the letter and I reported to the union how my guys felt about it. About 30 of us went to Johnstown one day and we picketed. We marched on City Hall. We circled the football stadium. We went to the Johnstown Labor Council. That was the extent of our picketing. Mr. Rooney took them up there to avoid any confrontation, and there was none. It was a classy move by Mr. Rooney.

The strike always seemed like it was close to ending and it was a really hard time because all four of our captains—Webby, Donnie, John, and Gary—had crossed the picket line. They were really good buddies of mine and they all apologized. But I understood and knew it might be their last season with the Steelers. I wasn't mad at them, but then questions came like: "How do you feel about Webby crossing the picket line?" I answered: "I'm more worried about the guys who are still out here on strike with me. I'm not worried about guys who have gone in." I avoided controversy at all costs. Bill DiFabio, a longtime radio reporter, would say, "Man, you dance better than Fred Astaire."

I had to be nimble after rumors started that teams were going to go cross the picket line and end the strike. At one point I asked our guys, who were striking, to hold out two more days, so if we didn't get a deal we would all go in as a team. I then got on an all-night conference call with Upshaw and the other player reps, and it turned out we weren't even close to a deal.

We met outside of Three Rivers Stadium the next morning, and I said, "If you guys want to still go in and we don't have a deal, we'll go in as a team. We'll stick together." But when I later talked to my agent, I told him I wasn't crossing the line. To me, it was a matter of keeping my word. I had made a statement at the beginning of the strike that as long as there was one guy out on strike, I was not going in.

My agent called Wolf and said, "You've got to talk to your boy. He's trying to make himself a martyr." Wolf called me, and I said, "I'm not trying to make myself a martyr. I'm just trying to do what I think is right and I don't think it is right to go in." He said, "Oh, c'mon, you've got to go in." I said, "Look Wolf, you can go in. I'm not going to be mad at you or disappointed in you. It's going to have no bearing on our friendship, but I can't go in." He said, "You're killing me." I said, "I'm sorry," and he said, "All right. You bringing the coffee or the donuts?" That was classic Wolf.

We met outside of Three Rivers Stadium the next morning, and the media was all there. Again, it was a secret meeting, but they were all there. The Steelers were getting ready for a game, and I gathered the players who were still striking and said, "Listen guys, I told you we'd be going in, but we don't have a deal. I'm going to be honest with you: I'm not going in without the deal. I made a statement and I'm sticking with it." I don't know if it was Robin Cole or David Little, but one of them said, "I'm not going in." Then one by one, everyone said they were not going in.

Less than 30 minutes later, I was on a conference call, and we voted as a league to go back in. The media was completely confused. I went to see Dan Rooney, and he said, "Tunch, you guys are coming in?" I said, "We are." He said, "So, how are you with that?" I said, "I've got to be honest with you. Forty-five guys went out with me. Now I know after these last two games, you're going to want to keep a couple of these guys, and I know not all 45 are going to be welcomed back. I'll be honest with you: that doesn't sit well with me, and I feel sick about it."

He looked at me and said, "How about this? What if we give everyone you come back in with two game checks and we'll tell you before we do anything. How are you with that?" I said, "That's more than fair. That's one-eighth of your salary." That was the deal, and I came away thinking, *What an honorable guy.* He didn't have to do that.

He was just a fair guy, and I can't reiterate that enough. At no point in my career was I ever worried about getting cut or reprimanded for being a player rep or later vice president of the NFLPA. If I disagreed with the Rooneys, I never felt that they were looking at me any differently. Mr. Rooney would never let stuff like that get in the way.

Wolf's Words

The situation was highly volatile. When you had Coach Noll saying, "I'll give everybody free agency. I'll cut them all." That's what you were facing. Being a player rep identified you as a guy who could be potentially highlighted around the league. It wasn't that way with Mr. Rooney, but for other guys who were player reps, that could be a bad spot. It really was a difficult time and it took a guy like Tunch, who has that personality where he is a real leader-type guy, to see us through it. He oozes leadership. He's always been that way since I've known him.

We only lost one game to the strike—they cancelled the third game of the season because the striking players returned too late that week—but I received quite an education. One thing I will never forget is talking to Art Rooney before the strike and the advice he gave me. He said, referencing his son and my boss, talking like we were contemporaries: "Tunch, you and Danny, you've got to influence the union and the league. We've got to do what's good for the game. I said that at the league meetings, and they looked at me like I was passé."

CHAPTER 13

The Rooneys

Art Rooney, the founder of the Steelers, had a mantra: don't be a big shot. I saw that mantra during my first encounter with the Pittsburgh icon, who was also known as "the Chief." It was right before the NFL draft in 1980, and Ted Walton, Nate Johnson, and I had been brought to Pittsburgh for physicals. We were at Three Rivers Stadium in the lobby. There were the four Super Bowl trophies and a mural of an AFC Championship Game against the Oakland Raiders, which had Gene Upshaw, Art Shell, Joe Greene, Jack Lambert, Jack Ham, all of these future Hall of Famers. It was behind the receptionist's desk near where we were sitting, waiting to meet Chuck Noll.

The Chief walked in and he was dressed very casually. He had on a cardigan sweater and he was missing a button, and part of his sweater was hanging out. He was chewing on a cigar and he had an empty ashtray in one hand and he was dumping the little ashtrays into the big ashtray. He said, "Hello, you fellas, what are your names?" We each introduced ourselves. Before Art Rooney could introduce himself, Johnson said, "So, are you the janitor here?" The Chief chuckled and said, "I do a little bit of everything around here."

I elbowed Johnson. *Don't you know who that is?* But it was so cool that the Chief was honored to be thought of as the janitor. He straightened up a little bit, and his chest inflated a little bit. He loved it. It was such a display of humility. You talk about being a regular guy. The Chief had a unique way of making you feel special, like you were his favorite. He made everyone feel that way.

I can't say enough good things about former Steelers president Art Rooney (on the right) and his son, then-general manager Dan Rooney, who pose for a photo in the 1960s.

He sent chocolate chip cookies to me in the hospital when I was in traction with a back injury. I didn't even know it was him. Ralph Berlin, the Steelers' longtime trainer, told me it was the Chief who sent those cookies over. What owner does that? I got a note from him in February one off-season from Canada and I was thinking to myself, *Who goes to Canada in February? People go to Florida.* The Chief wrote, "Up here in Ontario, having a great time. Hope you and yours are doing well." He was that kind of guy.

I took my oldest son, Tanner, who was about four years old at the time, with me to treatment on a Monday after a game. Tanner had this tennis ball, and the Chief said, "Hey, can you throw it to me?" Tanner handed it to him, and the Chief tossed it to him. Well, Tanner caught it, pivoted, and pelted it at the Chief. They were only about three or four feet apart.

The Chief reached out, but he almost lost his balance and almost fell to the ground when he caught the tennis ball. I thought, *Wow, pretty quick reflexes.* It was hilarious. I also thought, *Oh, this could be bad.* But he regained his balance—just like the athlete that he was—to avoid potential catastrophe.

The Chief was always in the locker room. He always came by to see how you were doing. He was just a great storyteller, and everyone loved to listen to him. Every time he walked by me in the locker room or the hallway, he said, "Tunch, my boy, how are things in Turkey? Are they still killing each other over there? Just like Ireland."

Dan Rooney, the Chief's oldest son and successor, didn't just turn the Steelers into one of the model franchises in all of sports. He also served as an ambassador to Ireland from 2009 to 2012. For some reason I could never call him anything but Mr. Rooney. One day he said, "Don't call me Mr. Rooney." I said, "Well, what should I call you?" He said, "Call me Dan, DMR, or Ambassador." I said, "Oh, okay, I think I like 'Ambassador.'" I started calling him Ambassador after that.

He was just like the Chief in that he was such a humble and regular guy. Tony Quatrini, head of the Steelers' marketing department, said that at the league meetings every owner would arrive in limos, and DMR would rent like a Bonneville or something uncool. When the Steelers and Green Bay Packers were in Dallas for the Super Bowl in 2011, there was a blizzard one morning. I still went out for my morning walk and I saw this elderly couple walking close to me, and there was a shawl over the two of them. As I got closer and closer, I realized it was Ambassador and Mrs. Rooney! I said, "Hey, what are you guys doing out on a morning like this?" He could have had a limo at his disposal, but he and Mrs. Rooney walked to mass and walked back in that blizzard. That was him. That's who he was. Someone had a great quote about him: "He walked with kings, but he was a man of the people." It's true, and his funeral in 2017 reflected that.

So many of my former teammates came back for it, as well as many dignitaries. Roger Goodell, Barack Obama, John Kerry, and Jerry Jones were there. Lamar Hunt's son, Clark, and Jerry Richardson also attended it. Mark Murphy, the president of the Green Bay Packers, brought a plane down because there were former Pittsburgh guys on the staff, including Dom Capers, Darren Perry, Ron Zook and Packers head coach and Pittsburgh native Mike McCarthy. They all came to the funeral as did Jason Simmons and Alex Van Pelt. There were people from the Rooneys' neighborhood there, too. That's what made it so cool. There was former President Obama and there were a bunch of guys who just walked in from the Oakland or the North Shore section of Pittsburgh.

That's one thing that makes this organization so unique. One of the old timers came to the Steelers' facility a while ago, and he asked, "So where is everybody's office?" *Well, DMR's is over there, and Art's is over there.* He said, "Art who? Artie, the ballboy?" It was hilarious. The cool thing to me is the current president of the Pittsburgh Steelers is a former ballboy.

Art Rooney Jr., Dan's brother, helped build the Steelers' dynasty with the great drafts in the 1970s. He is like the Chief: very outgoing, very gregarious, very gracious. Art was always very nice to me. He always said, "I knew you were going to be a good player. I wrote you up coming out of Indiana State." He told Craig Wolfley and I that each of us that had the highest Wonderlic score of our rookie class. We fight over that all the time.

We all battled with Ralph Berlin, the longtime trainer who was the best and a real character. If I got hurt, he said, "Oh, we better call Indiana State and get the alumni blanket to bury you in." He also said, "Tunch, you are on the ass end of a mediocre career," and "I was here when you got here and I'll be here when you leave."

He was just a ball buster, and I think his theory was that if he busted your balls enough, you wouldn't be in the training room; you'd be out on the field. He would be busting your balls, and you would give him a good zinger. If someone else in the room started laughing, he said, "You grin, you're in" and then he started on them. He always said, "I'm going to write my book, and all of you guys will start running for the hills." He also said, "Let me write you a prescription for sex when you get home. You're not getting enough, are you?"

One time I tore my rotator cuff and I wasn't practicing. Like an idiot I opened my mouth to the media and said something like, "I worked so hard. I was in such great shape to have this happen." Ralph taped the article to the doorframe as you went from the locker room to the training room at St. Vincent and said, "Oh, I worked so hard." I grabbed his lighter because he always smoked a cigar and lit the article, and the whole thing went up in flames. He said, "You're paying for the paint job! You're paying for the paint job!"

As much as Ralph busted our balls, he also really cared about us. When I came to a practice, I thought I had broken my finger because it had just swelled up. It ached, and I couldn't sleep. I said to Ralph, "Hey can you look at this? I don't remember breaking it, but it hurts." He looked at it and said, "Oh, man, that's a staph infection." He sent me to the hospital, and the doctors lanced it, and all of this puss came out of it. He knew what it was right away. When I got a concussion, he called me and called Sharon to check on us. He really cared.

Tony Parisi, a longtime equipment manager for the Steelers, was another character.

We were on the road my rookie season after I came back to the Steelers, and a buddy and I were having dinner in the hotel restaurant. He said, "Look at you. You were eating chili dogs, 50 cents apiece and hard-boiled eggs in Chicago when you were living on your buddy's back porch. Look at you now. You're eating shrimp and steak. Now you're living high on the hog. Don't forget where you came from."

Tony always had beer for us after the game. He turned the sauna off, and guys went in there and had a couple of beers. We even had visitors. Dave Casper came once. So did Bubba Baker and Jack Rudnay, the center for the Kansas City Chiefs. I don't know if it was Rudney or Casper, but one of them missed the bus to their airport and missed the flight home. He had to stay at Jack Lambert's house and take a flight the next day.

The Rooneys and people like Ralph and Tony weren't the only ones who made a mark on me. Chuck, of course, had the biggest impact on me, but plenty of other coaches also helped shape me. Rollie Dotsch, my first offensive line coach in the NFL, was totally old school and he coached you hard. To understand how tough he could be on young players, consider what happened at his Steelers farewell in 1982.

In the preseason it was known that he was leaving to become head coach of the USFL's Birmingham Stallions, and the Steelers had already brought in Ron Blackledge to succeed him. Blackie was with Rollie in camp, and at the end of camp, Rollie left. We had this dinner to say good-bye to Rollie, and Mike Webster, Jon Kolb, Larry "Bubba" Brown, and Steve Courson stood up at the table and gave toasts. It was coming to me, and I was like I'm not saying anything. I looked at Wolf, who was Rollie's whipping boy as well, and it wasn't like he jumped up and it kind of ended there. I regret that because he passed in 1987 after battling pancreatic cancer. In retrospect I know what he was doing, but it was too personal for me at the time.

One of the first times I drew his ire was my rookie year. I was coming around on a pull and I was trying to hit linebacker Dennis "Dirt" Winston, and Dirt blew me up. I was laying on the ground. The wind was knocked out of me, and I thought I had a hip pointer. Rollie stood over me and said, "That was horsecrap. You deserve to be hurt." He then just walked away.

Another time I was injured, and they were doing one-on-one pass-rushing drills. He said, "Tunch, go get a bag," which was the heavy bag that stood in for the quarterback. Then he started calling me a caddy. He would say, "C'mon caddy, bring the bag." I wanted to fight Rollie so bad. I got in a lot of fights my rookie and second year. Part of it was that in my mind I was fighting Rollie.

Plus, I knew that he liked the fighting. He always said, "You don't take any shit from anybody out there." To get in his good graces, you did what he wanted you to do. Phil Simms and I always talk about how we were coached as young players because he is the same age as I am. We agree that if today's player was coached like we were coached, they'd cry. With Rollie, I think part of it was being old school, and part of it was he was just trying to bring the best out of me. That was the way he did it.

Rollie had this way about him. There were a lot of opposing defensive players he disdained, and if you played bad against one of those guys, the animosity would get projected at you. In 1981 I had a bad game against Cincinnati Bengals defensive end Mike St. Clair, and Rollie was not his biggest fan. It wasn't enough that I got yelled at during the film session after that game. The next year in training camp, we were watching cut-ups from the previous season. Some of the plays against St. Clair re-surfaced, and I got yelled at all over again. Before practice that day after watching film, I was doing the hurdler's stretch, looking up at the sky, and all of the sudden, Rollie's face was looking down on me. He said, "I got one thing to say: Mike St. Clair." I said, "I'll get him next time Rollie." Rollie said, "You might not have a next time" and walked away. I think he was totally serious.

After the USFL folded, Rollie came back to the NFL and joined Green Bay Packers. In 1986 he came up to me after a game against the Packers at Three Rivers Stadium, gave me a big hug, and told me how proud he was of me. It was so encouraging. It made me feel like I finally earned my spurs with Rollie, something he used to say about veteran players. I'll never forget that moment.

Wolf and I swap Rollie stories all the time with longtime Steelers assistant head coach and defensive line coach John Mitchell. That's because Mitch coached for Rollie in the USFL. Mitch was his defensive line coach and he coaches a lot like Rollie. I'm going to quote Wolf here: "Mitch is a one-man Parris Island." Mitch coaches hard and he is going to break you and mold you into his image. Even though he coaches his guys hard, they want to play for him, and he knows what buttons to push. I start laughing when he is yelling at players now, and he will see me laughing and a lot of time he winks at me.

Mitch and I tell Rollie stories to one another and just crack up. He speaks so highly of him and he also speaks so highly of Bear Bryant. Mitch is one of the great men I've met in my life in part because of the trail he blazed in becoming the first African American to play football for Bear Bryant at Alabama. I met a guy who said that Mitch did so much for integration and unity on the Alabama campus just by being himself. He said that during a time of segregation and the time of the civil rights movement Mitch was just above the fray.

He told me this and literally started tearing up, and I can see why. Mitch is probably one of the classiest men I've ever met. He is one of the most interesting, too. He loves wine and traveling. He is so well-read, and his interests are so broad. If I ever want to go to a restaurant, I ask Mitch. I don't know if he considers himself a foodie, but I'll tell you what: he's given me some great calls on restaurants. I could talk to Mitch all day and never get bored. He's one of those guys.

So is Dick LeBeau, who was on Bill's staff my final season with the Steelers and was a longtime defensive coordinator in Pittsburgh. He might be the best defensive football mind I've ever been around. We were talking one time about how the zone blitz came into being, and he is largely credited with that innovation. This may or may not be an urban legend, but the story goes that Hall of Famer Dick "Night Train" Lane, LeBeau's teammate, was playing cornerback for the Detroit Lions on LeBeau's side of the defense, and he said, "Dick, cover my guy. I'm blitzing. They're not throwing to my guy at all." Dick said, "What do you mean, watch your guy? I've got my guy!" Lane said, "You can play them both." Dick ended up playing kind of a zone. So I asked Dick, "Is that how the zone blitz started?" He kind of smiled and winked.

Another time I was talking to Dick about Tom Brady, and he said, "Brady is fearless." When you watch film of Brady, one of the things you notice is that when he's in shotgun he doesn't look at the ball when it's being snapped. He's expecting the ball to find his hands and he's looking at the coverage already. We were talking about his ability to see the coverages, and you can tell that a guy is fearless on play-action passes by how quickly he turns around after faking the handoff. Brady will fake the handoff, have his back to the defense, and look like he is out for a walk in the park. He'll keep his back to the defense and then come out firing. Dick also said, "Man, the one thing about Brady is the distance from his hand to the receiver's is very short," meaning the ball gets there quick. I thought that was an interesting way to look at it.

Dick is just this gentleman and this genuine guy. When you're around him, you're better off. He's that kind of guy. Your day has been made better because of Dick. The same goes for Dick Hoak, the longest tenured coach in Steelers history. Hoakie joined Noll's staff in 1971 as a running backs coach and stayed with the Steelers through the Cowher era. It is easy to see why he had such longevity with one team. If you looked up *professional* in the dictionary, his face would be next to it. Hoakie was the ultimate pro and he enjoyed being part of the collaborative effort.

He could have had head coaching jobs or offensive coordinator jobs, but he was very content coaching the running backs. He was very content being here in Pittsburgh. Hoakie was just a great guy, and one of the things I loved about him, too, is that when he talked to us as offensive linemen he didn't yell. He would say, "Tunch, on this play understand what the running back is doing." He would come over and just kind of whisper it in your ear. It would be something like, "His release is going to be to the outside, so if you jump outside, you're going to get pinned." Or "He's going to give you a chip on this, so make sure you set accordingly." He was really good about helping you understand where the running backs were going, so that you could put yourself in a better position to block. One of the things that helped me understand what our running backs were doing was that Hoakie was so quick to share it with me. As a result, you were quick to say, "Hey, Dick, what's the back reading on this play?" I loved that about him, and that's what made him such a great coach.

Blackledge had a similar style and he could be characterized as the ice to Rollie's fire.

They were both teachers, but Blackie was an encouraging teacher, and Rollie was a coach-you-hard teacher. Blackie was a humble guy. We would talk about when he was the offensive line coach at Princeton, and he would say, "It's weird coaching guys that are smarter than you." When we were doing one-on-one drills, he said, "All right, we've got to set the tone. Ted, you're going to go first. You set the tone!" Ted Petersen went against Keith Gary, and Gary beat him on a quick swim move. Blackie threw his hat down and said, "That's not it."

Another time we were doing a drill, and Wolf threw an uppercut and tried to swim, and I threw him on the ground. He pulled me into a puddle with him, and we rolled around in it. Blackie just looked at us and said, "That's not what I'm looking for." He would just shake his head at us. He didn't get mad, but he would give this I'm-so-disappointed-in-you look. He was one of the most caring guys.

Blackie could really sing, and Todd, his quarterback son who was a teammate of mine on the Steelers, tells this great story about Frank Sinatra. Blackie loved Frank Sinatra, and he and Todd went to a Frank Sinatra concert at the Civic Arena in Pittsburgh. Blackie was singing every song along with Frank, and these two ladies in front of him turned their heads and said, "Would you mind? We'd rather hear him than you."

Tony Dungy never yelled to be heard and he spent a good part of the 1980s on Chuck's staff. I knew he was destined to be a head coach. He was so much like Chuck. Coach Noll looked like a teacher, but Tony looked even more like a teacher. The way he carried himself, you would think he was a professor, and when he stopped practice to make a point, he never raised his voice. Former Colts center Jeff Saturday told me a story when Tony first took over the Indianapolis Colts. Everybody was talking during his first meeting, and Tony waited patiently. Then it got uncomfortable because some people were still talking. Then everyone became silent. Tony said, "One thing you're going to find out about me is I'm not going to raise my voice. I'm going to talk to you at this level so it's important that you listen." That was Tony. He was the consummate teacher. He was just like Chuck without the edge.

His lips dripped with wisdom, and he just had this godly wisdom about him. He never let the circumstances of what was happening affect how he coached. That's what I truly admired about him. I don't think I ever heard him yell. Tom Moore coached for more than a decade on Chuck's staff and was the offensive coordinator for his last seven seasons in Pittsburgh. Tom is a perfectionist and he has this real gravelly voice. He actually sounded like Mr. Ed, but only when he said "run it again." He got on us because he wanted it to be right. He was a big KISS guy, but I'm not talking about the band. You always heard him say, "Keep it simple, stupid."

He took a lot of heat when he was the Steelers' offensive coordinator because people said the offensive was predictable. Well, the offense was Chuck's offense; it wasn't Tom's offense. Tom wasn't fired, but I think he saw the writing on the wall and resigned after the 1989 season. He will be the first to tell you that he learned a lot from Chuck, but in the end, he ran his own offense. We later saw that in Indianapolis with Peyton Manning and also with the Lions and Arizona Cardinals, where he also had a lot of success. He's a brilliant coach, a great guy, and had a great influence on Bruce Arians, the Steelers' offensive coordinator when Pittsburgh won the Super Bowl in 2008.

CHAPTER 14

Cowher Power and the End of the Line

A holiday gathering in 1992 showed me just how far I had come from the wide-eyed rookie who arrived in Pittsburgh in 1980—and how close I was to the end of my playing career.

Chuck Noll had retired after the 1991 season, and Bill Cowher had taken over as head coach. Bill and I are the same age, and we had played against each other. After Bill took over, he asked me about the team and questioned me about players and the culture in the locker room. I had never had that kind of conversation with a head coach. After playing for Chuck and that authority figure my whole career and then having a peer coach me, it was a very unique situation.

We had minicamp during the Fourth of July weekend. Sharon and the kids had gone to Indiana, and I was going to meet them on the fifth of July. I had nothing to do on the Fourth, and we had one more practice the next day.

Bill Cowher, who impressed me with his passion and attention to detail, hoists the Lamar Hunt Trophy after defeating the Indianapolis Colts to reach the Super Bowl in 1996.

So I went to a party that Bubby Brister threw, which had a big pig roast. When I walked in, everybody's head turned. It was like someone's parent had come to the party. I don't know if it was just my perception of how they viewed me, but I said, "Oh, man. Maybe it's time for me to move on." That's when I kind of knew it was my time.

Most of my buddies were gone. Craig Wolfley was gone, Gary Dunn was gone, Ted Petersen was gone, Mike Webster was gone. The only guys who were contemporaries of mine—and I really enjoyed their friendship— were Bryan Hinkle and David Little. When Wolf left as a free agent in 1990, Mike Mularkey started rooming with me. The year before Cowher came, Mularkey was going to retire. I told him, "You can't retire. If you retire, I'm not going to have anybody to hang out with." He came back, got hurt, and had back surgery. He's still cussing me out for talking him into coming back.

Even my favorite part of training camp in my latter years with the Steelers was a testament to my advanced age in football years. Mularkey and I had a TV in our room and by that time we had cable. Every night at 6:30 *Jeopardy!* was on. Hinkle, Brian Blankenship, Mularkey, and I gathered in our room. We had a little refrigerator so we had a couple of beers and "replenished our fluids." We played along with the contestants, and it got real competitive. You got a point for winning the game, and we kept a running tally all of training camp. Hinkle never won. The night meetings started at 7:00 PM, and the final question wasn't until five to 7:00. We waited until *Jeopardy!* was over and then zipped over to the meeting room. I guess that qualified as living on the edge in the latter part of my Steelers career.

I received another reminder that my time with the Steelers was coming to an end in 1992 when they took offensive tackle Leon Searcy in the first round of the draft. I didn't have a contract for that season, and when my agent called Mr. Rooney, he told him, "We won't have to get anything done until the end of camp." I basically got a pass on training camp. As Wolf said, "I got the Willy Wonka Golden Ticket."

You couldn't come to the camp without a contract, and Mr. Rooney basically said we'll get it done when it needs to get done. It was weird. It was the first camp I had ever missed in my career. I felt like I was playing hooky. I'm a worker and I'm always used to grinding. I talked Wolf, who had retired after the 1991 season following two seasons with the Minnesota Vikings, into putting his pads on and giving me some one-on-one pass protection work at Peterswood Park in Peters Township, Pennsylvania. We would be in this park, doing one-on-ones, and I'd throw him on the ground, and he would tackle me. We would wrestle because he was pissed off at me for slamming him. There were people having picnics, and they had to be saying, "What is wrong with those guys?" Imagine walking through a park and seeing two old men in shoulder pads and helmets with their hands taped up going after one another. It must have looked hilarious.

Wolf's Words

Only two people that I know have ever gotten the Willy Wonka Golden Ticket: Larry Brown and Tunch Ilkin. But Tunch was going crazy because he is a worker, and that's all we knew. He said to me, "Would you give me some pass rushes?" I said no because I had retired and dropped some weight already. I didn't want to put on the pads. I didn't want to put on the helmet. He probably asked four or five times before I decided to shut him up and just put the pads on. We warmed up, and I started to throw a couple of pass rushes on him and we picked up steam. We've always been competitive, and a lot of times that could boil over to extremely competitive. I got on the edge on him with an uppercut pass rush and I could see that he was starting to get honked off because he was not feeling like he was sharp. He had a great punch and could really knock you off your feet. He punched me really hard, threw me down to the ground, and then drilled me. I was pissed as all get out and I got up and smacked him in the head. I started headbutting him and bull rushing him, and we were cussing each other under our breath. There are those moments that you realize that whatever's going on is extremely stupid right when you're in the middle of it. You also realize that somebody is watching you. We stopped and turned around, and there was this group of people watching us. We had to look like these two idiots from a Bruce Springsteen "Glory Days" video.

After my contract got done, I reported to camp on the last day. At the press conference, someone asked, "Well, what were you doing?" That was the year of the Pittsburgh newspaper strike, and I jokingly said, "I tried out for town crier. I didn't make it."

We had a new staff, and Ron Erhardt was the offensive coordinator. He had always had big, giant offensive linemen with the New York Giants. I was always relatively small at 260 pounds, but I didn't look as small next to 275, 280 pounders, which is what I had been used to for most of my career with the Steelers. Well, I came into camp, and the left tackle was John Jackson at 310 pounds. Duval Love was the left guard at 330 pounds. Dermontti Dawson, the center, was 300 pounds. And the right guard was Carlton Haselrig at 310 pounds. Erhardt told me, "You're a lot smaller than I thought." I said, "I've been getting that my whole career." He said, "You might be too small to play in this offense." Obviously, I wasn't and I started at right tackle that season when I was healthy.

One thing I really loved about Bill was that he didn't try to be Chuck. He was totally his own guy. He was much more emotional, much more passionate. The spittle flying everywhere, the chin—all that stuff made him so interesting and unique. It was him. He wasn't trying to be somebody else. I really respected that about him and I'm not surprised he was successful. He had such a great attention to detail and he was ready for every situation. Bill was completely prepared and really impressed me with his organizational skills. He had this giant whiteboard with goals for every game. It was everything from first downs to yards rushing to sacks on both sides of the ball. I had never seen that before. His philosophy was that the season was broken up into four quarters, and you had to win three games out of every quarter, which would give you 12 wins and home-field advantage throughout the playoffs.

Bill showed his guts in his very first game when we played the Oilers in Houston.

We had a fourth down in our own territory, and he called a fake punt. He didn't hesitate, and Warren Williams, the upback, ran for a first down. That set the tone for the game and we won 29–24. Since I was the oldest guy on the team and a captain, I got to present him the gameball. I said, "We've got one gameball, and it's for his first win as a head coach, Bill Cowher." I always say I feel kind of honored that I gave Chuck his last gameball and I gave Bill his first gameball.

I broke my elbow against the New York Jets in the second week of the season and I missed the next game. Two weeks later we were playing the Green Bay Packers. I hadn't practiced, but I showed up at the pregame meal and said, "Hey, I can go." Bill said, "No, you're not going." I said, "No, no, no, you don't understand. I can go." He said, "No, *you* don't understand.

I'm putting you down." If you told Chuck you could go, then you would go. I thought, *Wait a second. I've never been told this before.* Bill must have seen the quizzical look on my face and he said, "Tunch, I don't need you today. I need you in the playoffs." I said, "Oh." The next week I was back with a big brace on, and he said, "You needed that." I had never experienced that before so it was a little different playing for Bill.

I also dealt with a hamstring injury that season, and it yielded a couple of funny moments. One game I was out in front on a toss sweep. I was running so fast, trying to get to the corner that I pulled my hamstring. It looked like a sniper shot me, and boom I went down. I limped off the field, and Bryan was laughing. He said, "That's what happens when you get old. That's what happens when you're 35 years old." He relentlessly busted my chops. The next series he went out there and pulled a calf muscle. They were helping him off the field, and I was howling. I said, "Sure, Hink, that's what happens when you get old! You blew your calf out. That's an old man injury! That's what you get when you celebrate someone else's pain. It comes back to haunt you!" I was laughing so hard.

We won 11 games that season and finished first in the AFC Central, which gave us a first-round bye in the playoffs. That year Neil O'Donnell suffered a hairline fracture to his leg, and Bubby started three games and played really well. We got into the playoffs and we had home-field advantage against the Buffalo Bills in the divisional round. Cowher started Neil instead of staying with the hot hand, and I know he still regrets the decision. Neil didn't play all that great, and we ended up losing 24–3 at Three Rivers Stadium.

I had a sense that game might be my last one with the Steelers. I was going to be 36 years old, and they had invested a lot in Leon. The exit interviews took place, and Bill told me, "Tunch, great year. Thank you. I appreciate you, but I think we're probably going to start Leon next year."

I said, "Just like that? It's not open? You're just going to give him the starting job?"

He said, "Tunch, we're paying him millions. We've got to find out if he can play or not. I'd like you to stick around as an insurance policy. I hate the word, but that's what you'd be. Your contract's done. This is the first year of free agency, you might get offers from other teams."

When the Packers offered me a deal, my agent called Jim Boston, the Steelers' chief negotiator, and said, "Hey, the Packers offered Tunch this contract. We haven't heard anything from you guys." Jim said, "Mr. Rooney thinks that Tunch should take that." I talked to Mr. Rooney, and he said, "Tunch, you'll always be a Steeler in my book." I call it the "thanks for the memories" speech. A lot of guys have gotten it, and that's why I went to Green Bay.

When I got to Green Bay, I looked at wide receivers coach Jon Gruden and I said, "Whose son is that?" He was so young. And then I saw Andy Reid, the tight ends coach. *How old is he?* And Steve Mariucci? I was looking at this staff and I had played against Nolan Cromwell, the special teams coach, and I played against Ray Rhodes, who was the defensive coordinator. I was way older than Gruden, older than Reid, probably a year younger than Mooch.

I joined the Packers the same year that the great Reggie White signed with Green Bay as a free agent. Reggie was the best I ever played against—and a source of both pride and enormous angst. He was your basic genetic mutation. Reggie could run, was athletic, and you couldn't get mad at him because he was the nicest guy ever. A lot of times when I played big, nasty players, I felt like David. When he was talking about Goliath, David's prayer was "Lord deliver this uncircumcised Philistine into my hands." With Reggie I said, "Lord, deliver this guy who probably loves you more than I do." He was so nice that you couldn't project any hate toward him. He would say,

"Hey, Tunch, how's the family? How have you been doing?" He was a great guy, and we were in Bible study together in Green Bay.

When I was with the Steelers and Reggie was with the Philadelphia Eagles, I watched film of him against Jackie Slater, a great offensive tackle who is in the Pro Football Hall of Fame. Reggie did a hump move against Slater, and it looked like Slater cartwheeled. The hump is when you throw the rip after the offensive tackle tries to put his helmet on you. Reggie was leaning in a way that Slater would come back with the club and Reggie could then use his momentum against him and throw him out of the way. Wolf said, "Damn, he levitated Jackie." Ron Blackledge, our offensive line coach, played it over and over and said, "Watch that hump. Watch that inside club."

That was Reggie's signature move. I was like *Okay, I've seen enough.* That move was in my dreams the rest of the week. When I played him, I always looked at that right shoulder because he tried to bull rush with the right shoulder; he tried to rip with the right shoulder and club with that right shoulder. I always focused on the twitch of his right shoulder. As soon as that moved, I tried to punch him in that right shoulder. When he bullrushed, I trapped his hands, and he went down because he was overextended.

The one thing I can say is I never gave up any sacks to him—not in the regular season, preseason, or even the Pro Bowl. But every time I played against him, I started getting nervous the Wednesday before the game because he was such a great player and would embarrass you. Mike Golic, who played with Reggie in Philadelphia, told me, "Tunch, you used to have Reggie talking to himself. He just couldn't figure out why he couldn't kick your butt." I was honored. That made me feel really good.

We were playing the Eagles one time at Three Rivers Stadium and we were playing from behind. Normally, Reggie went up against me, but one play he lined up against the right guard, and a defensive tackle lined up against me. We came to the line of scrimmage, and he was on Blankenship, who looked at me and said, "What's he doing here? He's supposed to be out there!" I said, "Why don't you ask him?" He said, "You're not supposed to be here! You're supposed to be on Tunch!" Everybody was cracking up.

Reggie and I had some great battles, and one of my best stories involves the Eagles and the great defenses they had with Reggie, Seth Joyner, Jerome Brown, Clyde Simmons, and Mike Golic. They were really good, and we played a very intense, physical game against them in 1989.

Merril Hoge got the ball on one play and he was going to the right. He cut left and when he cut to the back side Joyner was waiting for him and he just absolutely tagged him.

Merril came back to the huddle, looked at me, and said, "I think Seth Joyner just knocked the shit out of me." I said, "Yeah, that was a good hit." He said, "No, no, no, no. I mean he knocked the shit out of me." I said, "How do you know?" He said, "It feels like it." I said, "Turn around." He turned around and he bent over. I said, "Yep, you did." We were in the huddle and we were laughing, and that's what made football so great. You had these intense games, and then something funny would happen.

Merril untucked his jersey to hide the brown spot. The referee who was standing behind him said, "Merril, you're going to have to tuck that jersey in." Hoge said, "I can't." The ref said, "I'm going to have to send you off unless you tuck it in." Merril pulled up the jersey and bent over for the ref to see. He said, "Okay, you can leave it out." We were in the huddle just laughing. I said, "I'm sure glad I'm not Pinkie [the equipment manager] and have to wash those pants."

If it was a relief to play on the same team as Reggie in Green Bay, I received a flashback with the Packers' young quarterback, Brett Favre. He very much reminded me of Terry Bradshaw, who had told me, "I'm a gunslinger, I ain't a mailman." He had all of the confidence in the world in his arm. We were playing the Detroit Lions in the wild-card round of the playoffs, and it was the end of the game, and Detroit was ahead. Favre threw this rocket to the back of the end zone from the 50-yard line after scrambling around. Sterling Sharpe caught it, and that touchdown beat the Lions. It was Bradshaw stuff. After we beat Detroit in the wild-card round on Favre's incredible throw, we lost to the Dallas Cowboys in the divisional round.

My body fell apart that season. I kept pulling my hamstring and I pulled my triceps. I had knee surgery and wrist surgery. The player is always the last to know when it is time to leave the game. That year I played as a backup. I was initially a starter, but I got hurt, and then the Packers cut me because my hamstring wouldn't heal.

They brought back Tootie Robbins after he got cut from the New Orleans Saints, and then he got hurt. They called me back, but I could tell it was the end. We had moved to Green Bay and rented a place but only brought clothes and toys. When I got hurt, we all went home. I was back in Pittsburgh for four weeks and after the Packers called me back I stayed the rest of the season in a hotel because the kids were back in school in Pittsburgh.

I would go home after practice Monday morning and take the Tuesday night flight back to Green Bay. It was weird. I was in this hotel, missing my family and I was miserable, but I finished out the year. I came home after we lost to Dallas and I thought, *Do I want to play another year?* My agent called me and said, "Tunch, I've got two teams that are interested: the Jets and the Eagles." I was going to be 37, and there was part of me trying to justify another year. I thought there was something magical about playing 15 years in the league.

Then two things happened. We lost our youth pastor at my church, and before he left, he said, "Tunch, will you take the senior high ministry in the interim? Will you work as the youth pastor?" Then Mark Malone, who had been doing the Steelers pregame show on Channel 11, left for ESPN. I got a call from WPXI asking if I was interested in doing the Steelers pregame show and if I would test for it. That is how I got into broadcasting.

Men of Steel

Steelers who played the most years with the team (as of 2018):

15. Mike Webster (1974–88)
14. Ben Roethlisberger (2004–current)
    James Harrison (2002, 2004–12, 2014–17)
    Hines Ward (1998–2011)
    Donnie Shell (1974–87)
    John Stallworth (1974–87)
    Larry Brown (1971–84)
    Mel Blount (1970–83)
    Terry Bradshaw (1970–83)
    Ernie Stautner (1950–63)
13. Aaron Smith (1999–2011)
    Dermontti Dawson (1988–2000)
    Gary Anderson (1982–94)
    Tunch Ilkin (1980–92)
    Joe Greene (1969–81)
    L.C. Greenwood (1969–81)
    Jon Kolb (1969–81)
    Sam Davis (1967–79)
    Ray Mansfield (1964–76)

Hall of Fame Roll Call

The 13 Pro Football Hall of Famers who Tunch Ilkin played with during his 14-year NFL career:

Joe Greene
Jack Ham
Mel Blount
Terry Bradshaw
Franco Harris
Jack Lambert
Mike Webster
Lynn Swann
John Stallworth
Rod Woodson
Dermontti Dawson
Reggie White
Brett Favre

CHAPTER 15

The Press Box and Myron Cope

Working with Myron Cope was the best. It was like being around an old rock star. When Myron walked into a room, everyone ran to him. Women kissed him; men did imitations to him. It was a lot of fun. One of my favorite Myron stories involves a New Orleans Saints player named Fakhir Brown. *Fahkir* means poor in Turkish, and early in the game, I said, "Myron do you realize that Fahkir means poor in Turkish?"

He said, "Did you learn that at Indiana State?" He was always poking fun at the fact that I went to Indiana State. The Steelers scored a touchdown after wide receiver Terance Mathis beat Brown on a slant route, and Myron said, "Who is that guy, the cornerback who allowed it?" He then started to mispronounce Brown's first name and several times used a name that if you said it in front of your mother, she would wash your mouth out with soap. I was cracking up as Myron is calling him F---ker Brown and I finally said, while still laughing, "You can just call him Brown."

I have worked in TV and radio for almost 25 years and I think every ex-player thinks about broadcasting to a certain extent. I actually majored in broadcasting at Indiana State, but I was thinking behind the camera more than on-camera because I thought it would be easier to get a job that way.

O.J. Simpson was actually the guy who planted the seed of my becoming an on-air analyst. I did an interview with him in 1989, and after we finished he said, "Hey, Tunch, you ever think about getting in this business?" I responded, "Oh, Juice, like everybody else does." He said, "Well, you should do it. You're good at it. I'm not blowing smoke. If you want to do it, you should do it."

My big break came in 1994 when I still hadn't decided whether I was going to try to play another year. Mark Malone, my former teammate, had been doing the Steelers pregame show on Channel 11 in Pittsburgh, but he

When Bill Hillgrove (far right) and I were with Myron Cope (middle), it was like being in the presence of a rock star. (Pittsburgh Steelers)

left for ESPN. I got a call from WPXI asking if I was interested in doing the Steelers pregame show and if I would come test for it. I was still around 265 pounds, and my face was really fat. I saw it on the screen and said, "Damn, you guys are going from Tom Selleck to John Candy."

They offered me the job anyway, but my agent was trying to talk me into playing another year, so I was caught between the two. I asked Channel 11 if they could give me a couple of weeks, and they said sure, but they had to know soon because if I didn't want it they were going to give it to someone else. I was praying about it and I was thinking, *These broadcasting jobs are hard to find. They may not be available next year if I try to play another year. Do I really want to go to another camp at 37? Is my body really healthy?* I finally decided to hang it up and I started doing Steelers reports for Channel 11.

I got a call from NBC in 1995, and the network said I had been recommended to do color analysis. I tested for it, and NBC offered me the job. I did about 12 games that season and I loved working for NBC and learned a lot, especially from guys like Bob Trumpy. But I would leave on a Friday morning to do a game in Seattle or Buffalo and I wouldn't be back until Sunday night. I missed my oldest son Tanner's football games and my daughter Natalie's soccer games.

The year I started working for NBC, the Steelers hired Merril Hoge, my former teammate, to be the third guy in the booth for their broadcasts. I was like, *Oh, man, I wish I had known about that opportunity.* The funny thing is Merril wanted my job, and I wanted his job. When Merril left for ESPN in 1998, I called Joe Gordon, the longtime head of the Steelers' media relations department, and said, "Hey, are you going to put a third guy in the booth again?" He said, "We're thinking about it." I said, "Well, can I throw my name in the hat?" The Steelers hired me, and that's how I got into doing radio with Myron and Bill Hillgrove.

Our first broadcast together was the Hall of Fame game, and Myron and I each lived in Upper St. Clair. I said to him, "Hey, do you want to ride together? I can come get you." He said, "Do you mind if I have a smoke, dear Tunch?" I said, "No, my dad was a cigarette smoker." He said, "Why don't you drive my car?" I drove to his house and drove his car to the stadium so he could smoke. We stopped so he could have a toddy, which is what he called a drink, and we developed this rapport right away where we just had a lot of fun together. We had been very, very friendly during my playing days. I went on his show when he asked me and I knew his wife, Mildred. Working with him allowed me to interact with yet another legend.

I worked with Sam Nover when I first got into the business, doing the Steelers pregame show for WPXI. Billy and I worked together, and Stan Savran and I worked together. Myron made it my fourth legend of Pittsburgh broadcasting—at least on the football side of it—and it was a blast.

One time, Jerome Bettis made a great play, and Myron got so excited that he jumped off his chair. He conked his head on a TV monitor as he was doing the play-by-play and almost knocked himself out. I said, "Oh my gosh," and he said, "Oh, dear listeners, I hit my head and I'd like to take a moment to gather my thoughts."

At first it was intimidating working with Myron, but then we got real comfortable with one another. It's kind of funny because the first thing he said to me on our drive to the Pro Football Hall of Fame was, "This is how it's going to be: Bill will describe the play, then I will comment. If I want you to comment, I will look at you to bring you in."

After the very first play from scrimmage, he said, "That was a lovely tackle by the dear Levon. Do you not think, Tunch?" I wasn't waiting to get in that fast and I froze. All I was thinking was, *Myron, this is football. Why would you say a lovely tackle?* After that I thought we had a nice rhythm. Now there were times when I think I annoyed him because I jumped in too quick when I didn't think he was going to speak and then he did. There were times when he said, "Give me a pause, Tunch. Let me get my thoughts."

Myron really helped me and he always told me not to get too technical, and I know that's one of my faults. I get too technical because I love the game so much and when I see a scheme I will say, "Oh man, they're running the bear, and the Steelers aren't able to pick up the safety" or something like that.

Myron loved to argue, and he thought Tim Couch of the Cleveland Browns was a really good quarterback, and I did not. Before one game he said, "I understand that you do not think Couch is very good." I said, "No, I don't." He said, "Good, because we can have a nice argument." Well, Couch threw four interceptions that game. By the end of it, I said, "So what do you think of your boy Tim Couch now?" He said, "I…was wrong." Billy said, "Hold the phone, everybody. I've never heard that before." We had a lot of fun, and that has continued with Billy since Cope retired in June of 2005.

Billy is the best. He can paint a picture like nobody else. When we beat the New York Jets in the 2010 AFC Championship Game, he said, "And the only jet that's going to the Super Bowl is the one that's taking the Steelers." We were on the air when he said that, and I was just so amazed by that statement that I said, "Wow, that was really good." I had no comeback.

He is so eloquent, and I think that is because there is an artsy side to him. When we go on the road, he loves to visit jazz clubs and he knows where the best jazz club is in every city. He can sing, and I think that artistic bent is what makes him such a great play-by-play guy. There's always a portrait being painted when he does play-by-play.

Everybody loves Billy. Everybody in the city knows him, and he's a Pittsburgh guy. He's so gracious and affirming. I love working with him.

I've never felt he was angry at me except when I say, "Let's open up the windows," when it is real cold. He will say, "Oh…kay." I will say, "I will keep the window closed on your side, but I want to open it in front of me." Working with Billy is great, and I've worked with the greats in this city: Savran, Nover, Bob Pompeani, Guy Junker, John Fedko, almost every sports guy in Pittsburgh.

I am also teaming up with Craig Wolfley again after talking him into following me into the business shortly before Myron retired. I told him one day, "Why don't you get into broadcasting? You'd be great at it." He said, "I don't want to do it." He had his sports complex, and that took up a lot of his time, but I pitched it to Clear Channel Communications. I said, "We need a sideline reporter. Why don't we get Wolf? He's funny." Myron was very funny, and Wolf has brought that zaniness back into the broadcasts, following Myron's retirement. He is so good as a sideline reporter that the Steelers stuck with a two-man booth after Myron retired and kept Wolf on the field for games.

Shortly after Wolf joined me in broadcasting, we pitched a daily radio show, *In the Locker Room*, to Clear Channel. They didn't want to pay us, and we started our own media company, Tunch and Wolf Communications, and Steve Wayhart, an old friend of mine, sold it for us through his Brandmill company. That's how we got on the air for the first two years, and the show is still going strong.

I've learned from everybody that I've worked with, and so many of them have helped me. The two best bits of advice I got were from Trumpy and Matt Millen. My first game for NBC was with Trumpy and Tom Hammond, and Trumpy told me, "Tunch, take people where they can't go. Take them to the film room, take them to the huddle, take them to the locker room, take them to the bench. Get in the head of what a player might be thinking." I thought that was great.

Matty and I have been buddies for a long, long time, and when he was working for FOX, he had tried to get FOX to hire me. He told me after I went into broadcasting, "Don't listen to other people's opinions. Trust your own eyes. Watch film and make your own assessment of different guys. Everybody's pushing some guy for the Pro Bowl. You know football. Trust your own eyes." I thought that was a great bit of advice, too.

I watch a lot of film, not only for the upcoming game, but also for the show Wolf and I do together during the season, as well as for Steelers TV shows and appearances. On Monday of a typical week, I'll watch the whole game the Steelers just played and get a feel for the game I just saw. I get into the scouting room early and watch film from 8:00 AM to 10:00 AM and then I'll do the show and then I'll watch some more film before practice and then more film after practice. Thursday is my longest day of watching film. Friday I'll try to get into the facility early and go back to the scouting room and watch some more film. I will do my three keys to the game and then I'll do my radio show. I'll come in Friday morning, and Wolf will say: "Look at your eyes! What time did you get up to watch film? How much film did you watch last night?"

If I feel like I've watched enough film, I'll leave it at that. I normally don't feel that way so I'll watch some Saturday morning. If I'm watching the Cincinnati Bengals, and it's the second time around, I'm not going to watch nearly as much film because I've already seen them once and I know them. If it's a new team like the New York Giants, I watch a lot of film. I watch a ton of New England Patriots film because they fascinate me. I just try to pick up what they're doing because they always do something just a little bit different. The irony of that is against us in the 2016 AFC Championship Game they did the same thing as they had in their previous playoff game against the Houston Texans.

I try to talk to everybody—scouts, coaches, players. Everybody's got a different perspective based on their position, what they're coaching. I talk to the opponents' coaches, guys that I know. There are very few teams where I don't know a coach. On gamedays a lot of times you'll glean stuff on the field beforehand because I think people are a little more open. I'm looking to confirm what I already think I know based on what I've seen on tape. I will say, "This is what I saw. Am I seeing it accurately?"

The year that Denver Broncos quarterback Tim Tebow beat the Steelers in the wild-card round of the playoffs, Phil Simms was in Denver doing the game for CBS, and we've developed a friendship over the years. I stood next to him, watching Tebow warm up, and I learned something that I had never known. Tebow must have thrown a hundred balls warming up. The number of throws he made was obscene because nobody does that.

I said, "Phil, what's he doing?" He said, "Tunch, he's so amped up for the game he has to exhaust himself to get to the point where his release is the same every time. Watch his release. The release is different all of the time. His fundamentals are terrible, and he's trying to fatigue himself to be consistent in his fundamentals." I found that fascinating and I would have never known that because I'm obviously not a quarterback. I love listening to guys I'm going to learn from and I learn more from quarterbacks than anyone.

When I am analyzing a game, and Steelers left tackle Alejandro Villanueva gives up a sack, I'm not going to say, "Oh, man, Alejandro really stunk on that play." What I'll say is "DeMarcus Ware put a great move on Alejandro and had him on his heels." He did get beat, but he didn't get beat because he stunk. He got beat because the other guy made a great move. Or it will be, "Alejandro dropped his head and he didn't see Ware, and Ware got the edge on him." That's the way I critique guys.

I don't say guys stink. I have said, "Boy, that was a bonehead play." Plaxico Burress' brother called my radio show one time and complained that I was hard on Plaxico because of the time he spiked the ball after he fell down and wasn't tackled. I said, "What a bonehead play." But that truly was a bonehead play, and that's probably one guy who took offense to what I said.

I'm generally not a second-guesser of play-calling. Here is what I believe: those guys watch so much film and they're looking at match-ups. If a coach goes for it on fourth and 1, I'm not going to second-guess that. He's the coach. He's got a better insight to what's going on. If he calls a play-action pass because the safeties bit on the run fake, I've got no problem with that. Now on fourth and short, I'm a big quarterback sneak guy and I make that known. The reason I say that is because it's the easiest thing for an offensive lineman to block in short yardage. You cannot be wrong blocking because it's a wedge. Everybody goes hard to the inside so there's no questions about who to block, and you won't be afraid to miss. You will block somebody when you drive down hard to the inside. It's an easy block, and so I always go, "Run the quarterback sneak."

I don't tolerate the bashing of coaches on my radio show. When people are that critical, I say, "You don't know what you're talking about." When people say, "Fire Tomlin. Fire Colbert," I just say, "Wait a second, wait a second, wait a second." I know I've been accused of being a homer. Am I a homer? Well, I root for the Steelers. But I don't think I see the games in black and gold glasses. I see them pretty objectively.

If it's a bad call for us, I'll say, "Oh, we got away with that one" or "he missed that one." Every call that goes against the Steelers I don't think is a bad call. There are a couple of doofuses who call my show, but I do try to let everybody voice their opinions, and then I'll respond. I've been tougher on certain guys, but I think it's only when people call and are arrogant. If people call and just don't know what they're talking about, but they're nice people, I just say, "Okay, well, this is the way it really is." I'm not going to dismiss a guy because I think he's stupid. But I will dismiss a guy if he's stupid, arrogant, and opinionated.

As big as the NFL draft has become, I don't pay much attention to it and don't really have any media responsibilities prior to it. The draft to me is like a Cracker Jack box. You don't know what you're going to get until you open it up. You don't know if the prize will be a Green Hornet decoder ring or some goofy stamp. I don't know—and if I did know I could probably make a lot of money—why some guys transition to the next level so well.

It doesn't matter what school you went to. You could be from Ohio State or Southern Cal and lay an egg in the NFL. You could be from Indiana State or Valdosta State or Sam Houston State and become a player. I don't know why. I was a better college player than I was a high school player and I was a better NFL player than I was a college player. Why does that happen? I have no idea. People always ask me, "What do you think of the draft?" I just quote Chuck Noll: "They all look good in their underwear. They all look good in shorts and T-shirts running around with no pads." I don't analyze the draft because I'm unable to watch enough film on the players in it and I don't have access to the film that coaches and scouts have.

I really don't have to make any evaluations until training camp when I'm seeing it firsthand. For me to say: "T.J. Watt is going to be this or that or the other" isn't important. What's important is what I saw from T.J. when I watched him in training camp. I trust my eyes and I don't care what Mel Kiper, Jr. says. The guy has made a great living out of analyzing the draft, but I trust my eyes more than I trust his.

But I will say this: the best draft guy on television by far is Mike Mayock of the NFL Network. He is a great guy, and we've been buddies ever since he got drafted by the Steelers in 1981. Bill Hurley and I were in Three Rivers Stadium lifting a couple of weeks before the start of training camp that year, and Mike came into the weight room. We asked him what he was doing in Pittsburgh. He said, "I couldn't handle staying at home anymore." I said, "Do you have a place to stay?" He said, "No." I said, "You can stay with us" since Hurley and I were living together.

We hit it off, got to be buds, and have remained friends over the years. He was on the bubble with the Steelers as a rookie and got cut and went to the Giants and made the team. It was funny because the next season we played the Giants in the preseason, and I was the left tackle on the punt team. One of the guys Mike was competing against for a roster spot was lined up outside of me, and I had to block him. I got caught looking in right as the ball was snapped. He was upfield before I had even moved. I heard the sound that every guy on punt team dreads: thump, thump. It was my guy who blocked the punt, and I felt terrible. I said to myself, *I'm cut.* I saw Mike after the game, and we shook hands and embraced. He said, "Thanks for giving up a blocked punt to the game I am in competition with. Now he's got the edge on me."

Bill Cowher always coached on the edge and he made a successful transition to broadcasting after he retired in 2007. I am a little surprised he never got back into coaching. I knew that if Bill got back into coaching he was going to go to a place where there was a good quarterback and I knew there was a lot of interest in him so I was expecting him to come out of retirement at some point.

I think what happens with broadcasting is you realize: *Do I really want to go back to those kind of hours?* The game takes a lot out of you. When you grind and you grind and you grind, that's all you know. And Bill was a grinder. He was with Marty Schottenheimer, who expected his assistants to grind. Bill also has a Super Bowl ring so there's not a void there that might compel him to return to the sidelines.

It is an adjustment for players and coaches when they leave the game and go into broadcasting. After I finished my first game for NBC, I said, "Did we win? Did we lose? Was I good? Did I stink?" It left me very flat emotionally. That year I did one Steelers game, which I enjoyed the most, and I thought to myself, *This is kind of weird. I'm not invested.*

What I love about doing radio—and I think some fans take issue with this—is I want the Steelers to win, but I admire good football so I'll talk positively about the Patriots or Baltimore Ravens. I'm still emotionally invested enough to want the Steelers to win but not so much that I agonize over a loss like I did as a player. When you get out of the game, you do miss it, but I also think there is a steep price to pay when you play or coach. I am really happy with what I am doing, and having Wolf in the business and on the road really rejuvenated my desire for it. I always enjoyed broadcasting. I just enjoyed it a lot more after I had a brother to lock arms with—just like during our playing days. When Wolf and I are on the road, we can actually enjoy going out to dinner unlike our previous careers because we aren't so nervous about playing the next day.

But ask Wolf, and he'll say not all of our times on the road together are enjoyable. I love intense weather, and when we played the Miami Dolphins in 2004, they were evacuating the beaches because of an incoming hurricane. I said, "Wolf, we've got to go to the beach." He said, "We're not going to the beach." I said, "We're going to the beach." We went and Wolf and I walked the beach in Fort Lauderdale. Everything was closed, and it was the calm before the storm. It was so still. The clouds were so cool. Wolf said, "I think we need to get back." I said, "No, no, no, no. This is very cool." One of the things Wolf will say is I have talked him into more crazy things. I said, "Where's the hurricane?" I was getting impatient. Wolf said, "It's not coming so let's go back to the hotel." We went back, and that night the hurricane reached land, but it didn't hit Fort Lauderdale. It was still crazy with the wind and I said, "Let's go outside and walk around. Let's go see it."

Power lines were exploding, and you saw sparks and then light. People that were on the trip with us, including sponsors, said, "Where are you going?" I said, "We're going for a hurricane walk." Wolf said, "Don't ask me. I'm just going with him." We had about 10 people who took this walk, looking for the hurricane. The next morning we had a lot of time because it was a night game. I said, "I bet the waves are huge. Let's go."

We got to the beach, and the waves were just unbelievable. Wolf said, "You're going in?" I said, "Absolutely." The funny thing is the current was going north. Instead of giant waves that you could body surf, these waves went left and right. I knew it was safe because the current wasn't going out; it was going up. We jumped in the water, and it would take us 100 yards up the coast and we would run back and do it again. It was so cool.

Wolf's Words

I have no idea how he talked me into that. It was stupid. Who does that? Who goes walking in the middle of a hurricane? Who goes swimming in the ocean the day after it—when the riptides are crazy? But this is the stuff he gets me to do. One time we spent a whole day in San Francisco filming for Steelers TV, walking everywhere. You've got to understand that Tunch loves urban hiking; I'm not so inclined. We were doing this walking tour of San Francisco for Steelers TV, and I was getting more and more irritable as the day went on because the next night we were working the game and I had to walk the sidelines while he was up in the booth. He always has this way of convincing me that I want to do something, and I don't know how it happens. It used to be that I would argue, and somehow he would talk me into it. On this day we had probably done a good eight, nine hours of filming and walking, and I was like, I'm done. He said, "We've got to walk across the Golden Gate Bridge." I said, "Are you out of your mind?" I was shouting at him. I was so mad, and it takes a lot to get me mad, but I lost it. There was no way he was going to make me or fool me into thinking I wanted to walk across the Golden Gate Bridge.

I love stuff that borders on or crosses into the extreme. Ted Petersen, Leo Wisniewski, and I used to take all sorts of father-son trips together and we have hiked all over. My sons, Tanner and Clay, and I went to Colorado one year with Ted and his sons, Garrett and Teddy. We took an RV, and everything went wrong. I bent the key real bad in the ignition at one point and I didn't tell Ted so he broke it off. We took the dashboard off and we just kept hotwiring it the rest of the way. The air conditioning broke, too, but we had a great time.

Two years later Jon Kolb and his sons and my sons and I went rock climbing at the Garden of the Gods in Colorado. Kolby can rock climb, and his sons are great climbers. We hiked to this place called the Lake of the Clouds, and it was straight up six or seven miles. We hiked to the summit, and all of the sudden, this storm came in.

Kolby and his sons had already started back down, but I was just fascinated about being up there. The storm coming was eye level, and I was just standing there. Clay said, "Hey, Dad, don't you think we should get down?" I said, "Wait a second. I want to watch this." He said, "Dad, don't you think..." I said, "Wait a second. This is very..." He said, "*Dad* we're on a mountain, and there is a lightning storm coming in. Don't you think we should go down?" I said, "Good point."

CHAPTER 16

The Right Path Taken

B roadcasting has allowed me to stay close to football, and the blocking technique I am best known for has given me an opportunity to do some coaching. Jim McNally, who was the Cincinnati Bengals' offensive line coach and was always very complimentary to me when we played the Bengals, called me after I retired in 1994. He was with the Carolina Panthers then and said, "Hey, I'm looking at your video, your Tunch's punches video." I said, "Tunch's punches? Oh, that was one of my workouts." He said, "Can you come teach my guys?"

That's when I started doing it, and I've worked with teams every year since I retired with the exception of the lockout year in 2011. After going to the Panthers first, I worked with the Indianapolis Colts second because Ron Blackledge, my position coach with the Steelers, was the offensive line coach there. Bobby Ross brought me to the Detroit Lions three or four years in a row, and that's where I met current Steelers general manager Kevin Colbert and former Steelers college scouting coordinator Ron Hughes.

I've probably worked with more than half the teams in the NFL and a bunch of college teams as well. People just started calling it "Tunch's punches," and I did a video. I've worked every year with at least one team and sometimes two or three. I've worked with the Steelers too, including guys like current starting left tackle Alejandro Villanueva, Jamain Stephens, Paul Wiggins, and Tom Myslinski.

I had several opportunities to go into coaching after I spent my final NFL season with the Packers. Before I left Green Bay at the end of the 1993 season, Mike Holmgren said, "Thanks for coming out here for a year, but we're not going to bring you back. Tunch, would you like to coach? Because if you would, I would love to have you. You may just want to get away from the game for a little bit. If you decide you want to coach, let me know." His wife said the same thing to Sharon. She said, "If you're interested, tell Tunch."

Even though I passed up a coaching offer from Bill Cowher, I still give pointers to linemen—like the great David DeCastro. (Pittsburgh Steelers)

Mike would probably be mad at me for telling you this, but he's spoken about him like he'd like for him to coach for him."

Ross and later Matt Millen wanted to hire me, too. When Matty took over as president in Detroit, his dream was to have current Steelers offensive line coach Mike Munchak and me—Munch as the head offensive line coach and me as the assistant—on the staff. Sharon said, "Look, if we go somewhere, I'm not going to know anybody. I'll go with you anywhere, but just know that if you go to Detroit, it's going to be a lot harder on me than it is on you." I said no both times to the Lions.

My career path almost veered into coaching full time in 1999 when Bill Cowher asked me during the season, "What are your broadcast responsibilities?" I told him, and he said, "So, you couldn't coach right now?" I said no. He said, "Kent [Stephenson] is getting up there. I'd like you to coach with him one year and then I'd like for you to be the head offensive line coach."

I started praying right away. I said, "Lord, is that what you'll have me do?" I prayed. I fasted. Why fast, people may ask? Because in the Old Testament, people fasted for clarity. Fasting is one of the disciplines of the faith. The disciplines are memorizing scripture, reading scripture, praying, and fasting. If you remember the Sermon on the Mount, Jesus said, "When you fast." He didn't say, "If you fast." When he was trying to get clarity from God, Daniel fasted. There is a history of God's people fasting, so I fasted.

I guess I was waiting for a neon sign, but I never got it. The elders at our church are really good friends of mine, and I asked them, "What do you guys think?" They all said the same thing: "Tunch, if you feel like you are being led to do it, do it. If it doesn't work out for you, you can get out of it." The season ended, and Bill said, "Hey, I want you to come see me."

I met with him, and he offered me the job. He said, "I want you to meet with Kent." Stephenson told me, "I'd love to work with you." Bill was real excited, and I said, "Give me 24 hours. Let me go home, process this." If he would have pressed me, I would have said yes. In his presence I was leaning toward taking it because he is very passionate and he is a good salesman. The farther I drove away from Three Rivers Stadium, though, I said, "I can't do this."

I don't know why, but when I got home, I walked in the door and said, "Sharon, I'm not going to take the job." She started crying because she had told me to take the job, but she really didn't want me to do it.

Three years later she got sick. She was diagnosed with breast cancer, so I know the Lord was preparing me for it because I couldn't have gone to every chemotherapy session, every radiation, every doctor's appointment if I had been coaching full time. The eight years she was sick, I might have missed one or two of her appointments but not many, and my mind wasn't somewhere else. If I had been coaching, I don't know if I could say that because the game is so consuming.

It was crazy because she had a small tumor, no lymph involvement, and her margins were clean, which meant it didn't look like the cancer had spread to other areas. She should have done well after her first round of chemotherapy, but six months after her chemo was over, the cancer came back aggressively. There was more surgery, more chemo, more radiation, and it came back again.

Sharon went to this place called Healthquarters Ministries in Colorado Springs. She did seven-day fasts every five weeks and she was doing really well. But when the Steelers played in the 2010 Super Bowl in Dallas, she developed this cough. She said, "My cancer's back." We went to the Hillman Cancer Center in Pittsburgh, and, sure enough, there were several tumors on her. They operated, and in May after chemo and radiation, the cancer was gone. We just praised God and gave thanks.

We went on summer vacation to Rehoboth Beach in Delaware, and at the end of it, she said, "My cancer's back." She just knew. We got home, and she was right. We went to Tijuana, Mexico, and we were down there for a month. The Steelers let me take off from doing the games so we could try some experimental medicine. We almost lost Sharon down there. She had brain and spinal tumors. We came back, and she was in and out of the hospital for the last six months of her time here on Earth. On February 6, 2012, the Lord took her.

It was such a rollercoaster ride. She would get to death's doorstep and she would rally. Her oncologist—a great guy, who I love—finally said, "Tunch, she's not going to rally this time. There's just so much cancer in her lungs."

She was in a wheelchair from October until February because of the tumors on her spine. We had family around us during that time. Sharon's mom lived with us, my mom was there all the time, and we had our friends and our church friends. Our church family was so gracious. That last year— at least the last six, seven months—I don't think we cooked a meal at our house. Whenever she was getting chemo, the meals started coming. I would tell Cheryl Colussy, one of Sharon's best friends, "Cheryl, we're feeling a little guilty about this." She would say, "Tunch, do not deny these ladies this blessing. They want to bless you guys. Don't feel bad about it. Just receive it."

Guys came to the house and prayed all of the time. They also came to the hospital to pray. Craig Wolfley, Jon Kolb, and Leo Wisniewski were all in the room with me on the second-to-last day before Sharon passed. My pastor was there, guys from my men's huddle were there, and guys from our leadership team in our men's ministry were there. Before the viewing a bunch of my guys from the church said, "Hey, we'll stay at your house." I said, "Why are you going to stay at my house?" One of them said, "Because people get burglarized." I never heard that. I said, "Who would be that much of a dirtbag?" He said, "It happens all of the time."

When Sharon passed, we still had 100 Oxycontin pills, and because of my drug background, a voice said, "I know how to kill the pain." I looked at the pills and said, "Who could blame me? My heart is broken. Who could blame me? And who would know?" I even told the Lord, thinking back to when Sharon and I made an agreement to not drink anymore, "Hey Lord, that was a three-way covenant. You took Sharon; you broke the covenant."

But the Lord saw right through that. He said, "Tunch, you know I love you, and my grace is sufficient." Just like he told Paul, "In your weakness you will find my strength." I didn't hear those words, but my heart, which knows the word of the scriptures, came flooding back into my mind. I dumped the pills down the toilet and flushed them.

When you go through pain like that, you feel like you are entitled. My senior pastor and I are really good buddies, and he said, "Are you all right?" I said, "No, I'm about to lose it. I'm about to leave town, go down to the Florida Keys, and become a Jimmy Buffett song." It was a joke. I couldn't go off the deep end because I knew the consequences, but a part of me wanted to do it. That's where locking arms with my brothers in the Lord comes in because my brothers had me surrounded, and they were watching out for me. They were praying for me and they all came alongside me for support.

I didn't want to bring shame onto the Lord or my family, but there was part of me that just wanted to go crazy. But I had my buddies praying for me, and I think telling them that made them pray for me more intensely. Wolf was really worried about me. He was looking to bring me some joy, and that's why he introduced me to Karen. We were in Mexico doing a football clinic with James Harrison, Emmanuel Sanders, Charlie Batch, and Ryan Mundy, and some others, that summer.

The first night was the sponsor's event. Wolf brought this woman over to me and said, "You've got to meet this girl. She lives across the street from your mother on Mount Washington." We met, and she said, "How are you doing? My name's Karen Rafferty. I work for GM. I'm the director of advertising and marketing here in Mexico." She was from Martins Ferry, Ohio, but had lived in Pittsburgh several times.

She said, "I was so sorry to hear about your wife, Sharon. I read about her in the paper. I lost my husband, too." We got to be friends, and I always said if I got married again, it would have to be someone who is a Christian, someone who didn't have children, someone who was within 10 years of me—she's seven years younger than I—and she checked all of those boxes.

We talked for the next six months on the phone every night, and she put in for a transfer. We dated when she got home and flew down to Costa Rica and got married on March 17, 2013. Wolf was responsible for that, and at a get-together, he said, "Tunch, for the longest time, you looked like a raisin. Now you're starting to look like a grape." Leave it to Wolf to put it so eloquently.

She suffered loss, and I suffered loss. The Lord brought us together, and I think we healed each other's hearts. The funny thing is Karen is a huge Steelers fan. Martins Ferry is only about 60 miles away from Pittsburgh, and she listens to Wolf and me every day on our radio show.

All three of my kids live in the Pittsburgh area and all three were active in sports. Tanner, my oldest, was a boxer. He used to box out of the gym Wolf owns and he was good enough to win a Pittsburgh Golden Gloves championship. He kept boxing at the amateur level until his neurologist told him to stop. He married Jessica Stripay in 2013, and they have a son, Levi.

Natalie was a soccer player and she had a chance to play collegiately, but I think she had enough soccer and she went to Virginia Tech. Natalie never had any interest in football, but one day over Christmas break, she said, "Hey dad, are you watching football tonight?" I said, "Huh?" She said, "Do you want to watch football together?" I said, "Who are you and what did you do to my daughter?" That's when I found out she was dating Danny Coale, who played wide receiver at Virginia Tech and got picked in the fifth round of the 2012 NFL Draft by the Dallas Cowboys. He also spent time on the Indianapolis Colts' practice squad.

Danny never missed a game in four years at Virginia Tech, and it was like all of the bad luck hit him when he got to the NFL. He was on the Cowboys' injured reserve list and was with the Steelers one training camp, but he shattered his finger and had it surgically fixed. He came back at the end of the season on the practice squad. He bounced around and was on several other practice squads for a while. He and Natalie also got married in 2013, and they have a son, Abbott. Danny works at PNC Capital Markets.

Clay was the football player of my kids. He played at Upper St. Clair High School and tried to walk on at Ohio University but didn't make the team. When Sharon got real sick, he enrolled at Robert Morris University so he could be at home. He walked on at Robert Morris and he got some playing time on special teams and as a nickel defensive back. Clay coached three years at Geneva College and just found that he could make more money with better hours in construction.

Tanner owns a construction company, and Clay has been a big part of it. Tanner is the craftsman and Clay, who also has his real estate license, is the marketer and business man, and they love working together. Clay married Kristin Yoviene, a former lacrosse player at Robert Morris, in June of 2018.

Our kids were always close, but what we all went through with Sharon brought us even closer together as a family. I love being a grandpa. Karen and I will take the kids overnight, and they're just a blast. Spending time with my family is a daily affirmation that I made the right decision when I bypassed a career in coaching. I've asked Mike Mularkey and other buddies who went into coaching what it was like. They all said there is a price to pay, and you have to love coaching.

I got to coach both of my sons' teams in youth football and I watched my daughter play soccer. I didn't miss anything. And you know what? I get to coach up men in life. I've been the men's pastor at South Hills Bible

Chapel since 2005, and we have five campuses. I teach a class on Wednesday nights called "The Locker Room" and everything I teach at a foundational level is growing in Christ, what it means to be a man of God, and what it means to be a godly father and husband.

We have a 16-man leadership team, we meet every other week, and we've got all sorts of outreach activities to draw men into the church. We work out together and we have a weight room in the lower level of our church with all the machines you could ever want. The philosophy is to create a third-place environment for men. Men need a home. Men have to work, and everyone needs a third place. Why not the church?

I counsel guys, and sometimes it's just a guy struggling with things. Sometimes it's getting a guy connected with Bible studies because we have them every day of the week. I also speak at a lot of churches and men's groups in the area and around the country and work with our peer mentor program. I think it's safe to say that I've got a pretty good coaching gig.

CHAPTER 17

Finding My Way

In my heart I want to minister with men. That is my passion in life. I know Jesus and I know football. My love for Christ and my passion and love for men is what drives me. Football has become a platform that the Lord has given me to do those things. I use the football format for my men's ministry. Christ is the focus, and camaraderie is the way to encourage and challenge men. Competition is the way to get men to open up, and confidentiality is at the core. I call it the "four Cs"—Christ, camaraderie, competition, and confidentiality. On a Wednesday night at ministry, we will start off with trivia. The classes are roundtables so I'll start the first part with table questions. I'll do three Steelers trivia questions or three NFL trivia questions and then three open Bible trivia questions, and you get points. Then I'll teach a lesson.

I was raised a Muslim, and that is not the only reason why I might be as unlikely a Christian as I am a devout one. I grew up in the 1970s and was a product of it. I started doing drugs in high school and got high for the first time at a Sha Na Na concert. I started with pot and when I got to college I experimented with all kinds of drugs—something I'm not proud of.

In addition to broadcasting for the Steelers, I am a minister, a role to which I'm very devoted. (Pittsburgh Steelers)

The French philosopher and scientist Blaise Pascal said something about how, "There is a God-shaped void in every man, woman, and child. It can only be filled by the person of Jesus Christ." I was trying to fill that void with drugs and being wild and fighting and football. I wasn't disrespectful or rebellious, but I loved to live on the edge. Everything that would shrivel up your nuts—whitewater rafting, rock climbing, drugs—I wanted to do. In that sense I guess I was rebellious.

I fought a lot. That's the way I was. My buddy Leo Wisniewski, who played for Penn State and the Colts, says that I have the immigrant chip on my shoulder, which is probably true. I was trying to show everyone that I belonged and was tough enough. When I came to the Steelers, I met a bunch of guys who loved Jesus, who loved each other, and who loved me. I had never seen guys like this. I saw Mike Webster and Jon Kolb, Donnie Shell, and John Stallworth, and those guys had such a purpose.

Before joining the Steelers, I thought Christians were weak. I thought they were effeminate. I thought they were weenies. I wanted no part of them. In college there was a group of them that met. It wasn't that I avoided them; I was just oblivious to it. In retrospect I see that the Lord was chasing me. I went to chapel once my senior year, and that was the first time I heard the message of the cross, that Jesus loved me, that He died on a cross for me, that He paid the price for my sins, and that He did what I could never do for myself. I said, "Wow, that's interesting." Then a bodybuilder I trained with in the offseason of my senior year said to me one day, "I'd like to talk to you about Jesus. Would you listen to me?" I said, "Sure."

He gave me the message of the cross. He said, "God is holy." I said, "I get that." He said, "We are sinful." I said, "I have no problem understanding that." He said something had to be done to bridge the gap between sinful man and a holy and righteous God, and that is Jesus on the cross. I said that kind of made sense. Later I was on spring break in Daytona Beach, Florida, and Campus Crusade was down there, and another guy told me about Jesus. Normally, I tuned those guys out. But I listened, thought it was kind of cool, but that was as far as it went.

When I got to the Steelers, that message continued, especially through Webby, Kolby, and Craig Wolfley. On the plane ride back from Oakland, which turned into a seminal moment near the end of my second NFL season, Webby informed me that Jesus stands at the door of my heart and knocks, and if I ask him in, He'll come into my life. Webby told me that all who have sinned have fallen short of the glory of God, Romans 3.23, and then Romans 6.23. The wage of the sin is death, spiritual death, eternal separation from God. But the gift of God, he said, is eternal life. *Could it be that simple?* That's the question I kept asking myself.

That winter, Wolf and I were doing a youth football banquet, and Wolf's dad was dying of leukemia. I asked him, "How are you handling this? It's got to be tough thinking about losing your dad?" He said, "Tunch, my dad loves Jesus, and the moment he closes his eyes here on Earth, he's going to wake up in heaven in the presence of Almighty God. Not because my dad's a good guy but because of the cross of Christ."

I said, "How do you know that?" He said, "Because the testimony is this of first John. God has given eternal life. This eternal life is in his son, Jesus. He, who has the son, has eternal life. He, who does not have the son of God, does not have eternal life. John, in his first letter, said, 'I will tell you this, so that you may know that you have eternal life.' So I know my dad's going to be in heaven, and heaven is unbelievable. It's more beautiful than the greatest beauty of the Earth." He then said, "Tunch, it's just a simple prayer. It's not magical, but it is. You're submitting to Christ. You're admitting that you're a sinner. You're admitting that you need a savior and you're admitting that Christ died on the cross for you and now you're saying I'm going to follow Him. Tunch, would you like to pray to receive Christ?"

It was anything but a simple question. The worst thing you can do as a Muslim and a Turkish Muslim is become a Christian; you are now an infidel. I was thinking my parents would freak out and I wondered what I would tell my old buddies. Then I thought, "I'm going to be one of those weirdos." Wolf again said, "Would you like to pray and receive Christ?" I said, "No, man that would be too weird. I need some time to think about it." He said, "Well, don't wait too long. I'd hate for you to die before you have that chance."

All of these people that God put in my life were telling me about Jesus. Then I picked up this book called *The Late, Great Planet Earth* by Hal Lindsey. It's about the end of times, and I was very interested in what I now know is eschatology, which looks at the afterlife. I read the book, and at the end of the book, Lindsey gives the salvation message and he gives you an opportunity to respond. He said if you feel God is tugging on your heartstrings and that you ought to give your life to Christ, it's a simple prayer, and the prayer is in the last chapter of the book.

I said the prayer and I looked around. I was waiting for something to happen, a lightning bolt, God's voice, something. Nothing happened, and the next day I went to work out. It was the offseason, and I said, "Hey, Wolf, guess what I did last night?" He said, "What?" I said, "I gave my life to Christ." He and Kolby were so happy, and it really struck me. I knew what I had been doing in my life was not getting it done for me, that there had to be more to life than that. I wanted meaning and I didn't have it.

That was when my journey started. It wasn't like I changed just like that; it was a growth process. The first thing I thought was how am I going to tell my parents? I saw Sharon that weekend and said, "You'll never believe what I just did." She said, "What's that?" I said, "I gave my life to Christ. I became a Christian." She said, "What does that mean?" I said, "I don't know, but it means I'm not going to hell and I'm really happy about it." She was a Catholic, so initially I think she was kind of thinking let's see what this is all about. Then she saw the change in me. Slowly but surely I cut the drugs out of my life, quit acting like an idiot, started reading my Bible all the time.

My mom came to visit soon after I accepted Jesus Christ and she is very perceptive and sensed something. She said, "You changed your religion, didn't you?" It was out of nowhere, unbelievable. I said, "How did you know?" She said, "I had this dream that I'm chasing you. You're in a church and you're saying, 'I've found my way. You've got to find your way.' I failed as a mother. How could you do this to us?"

I was doing an autograph session that day with John Goodman and Bobby Kohrs at Bull's Tavern in Ligonier, Pennsylvania, and we were staying overnight because we were going shooting the next morning. Sharon called me and said, "You've got to come home right now. Your mom's freaking out." I didn't have a car because I had ridden up with either John or Bobby. I said, "Well, these guys aren't going to leave." She said, "We'll come and get you," and they did. We hashed it out on the way home and talked about God's mysterious ways.

He had put a very bold, young Christian Turkish woman named Aylin in her life, and Aylin was telling everyone about Jesus because all of her friends and relatives were Muslim. She was going to convert the entire Turkish population of San Francisco and bring them to Christ.

My mom was trying to figure out what happened to her son, and she said, "I'll go ask Aylin." Meanwhile, a missionary sent me a Turkish New Testament bible, which I sent to my mom. She started reading about Jesus and she was very intrigued. In the process she went to church with Aylin. My mom had another dream and in this dream she saw Mary with the baby Jesus in her arms, giving Him to my mom. My mom said, "I can't," and Mary said, "Well, he's for everybody."

My mom didn't know what that meant. She thought that meant Sharon and I were going to have a baby. I said, "If that was truly God coming to you in a dream, that means Jesus is for everyone. He died for the world." My mom ended up giving her life to Christ, and then we tried to figure out how to tell my dad.

This, I knew, was going to be a lot harder than telling my mom. Recent history had told me that. When Sharon and I got married, we exchanged our vows at St. Gabe's Catholic Church in Connersville, Indiana. My father had initially said, "I will not come to the ceremony." I said, "What do you mean you're not going to come to the ceremony?" He said, "I can only come to the reception. It is against my honor." I said, "What do you mean it's against your honor?"

Turkey is an honor/shame culture, and the best thing you can do for your family and yourself is to bring honor. The worst thing you can do is bring shame, so in his mind, going to the church would have brought shame. I had to broker a compromise to get my dad to change his mind. A buddy of his—I called him Uncle Sacip—was kind of a Muslim cleric, and he read the Koran. That led to as interfaith a wedding ceremony as you can get. My best man was Jewish. We were married by Sharon's uncle, Father Dave, and Uncle Sacip was there with the Koran reading in Arabic. Nobody understood what he was saying—even the Turkish people there. I sat there saying, "What's wrong with this picture?"

Consider that backdrop when I say how scared I was to tell my dad that I converted to Christianity. My dad was only 5'7", but he still intimidated the hell out of me. Good man. Hard worker but a tough guy. He was very proud, stubborn as a government mule, and a guy who would have no trouble destroying relationships. I said, "Lord, you've got to do this."

Every time Sharon and I visited my parents in San Francisco, I tried to tell him, but I chickened out. Every time they came here to visit—for about four years—I chickened out.

They came to visit us around 1986, and we were playing the Cincinnati Bengals on Monday night. I said, "I'm going to tell him this weekend." My dad had undergone bypass surgery after a heart attack, and I didn't want him to die without hearing the truth.

I took him to practice with me on Sunday and I was going to tell him on the way there, but I chickened out. I said, "I'm going to tell him on the way home," and I chickened out again. We were going home to watch the Chicago Bears-Dallas Cowboys game, and I said, "I'm going to tell him during the game." As we watched the game, I said, "I'll tell him at halftime," but I kept chickening out.

Then my dad out of nowhere looked at me and said, "Hey, how come you never told me you became a Christian?" I said, "*What?*" He said, "How come you never told me you became a Christian?" I said, "I was afraid of how you would react." He said, "You know me, I'm one of those liberal guys. I think that's great." I thought, *No, you're not one of those liberal guys.* I said, "How did you find out?" He said, "I read it in the program."

Lynn Molyneaux had written an article for the Steelers' gameday program on me, and my testimony was in that article. I had hidden that program in my den, so he had to have been snooping to find it. The Lord did it, and so now it was open season on my dad. I gave him a Bible. I prayed for him and I let him hear me pray for him. I gave him a pocket New Testament, and he carried that everywhere.

I got a letter from him in 1990. It said, "I'm out fishing in the San Francisco Bay. I'm not catching any fish, but I'm reading the Bible you gave me and I'm reading about the Beatitudes. I'm thinking what can I give my son that would be meaningful this Christmas? I thought the best thing I could give you is joining you in your faith in Christ."

In 1994 I moved my folks out to Pittsburgh after I retired. Ron Moore, our senior pastor at South Hills Chapel, said, "Tunch, how can I minister to your parents?" I said, "I think my dad got the real deal. Go find out for me." He shared his life story with Ron, and I didn't even know this, but my dad was always looking for God. He said, "I didn't find it in Judaism, I didn't find it in Islam, I didn't find it in Catholicism. I felt like the Robert Frost poem, 'Water, water everywhere but not a drop to drink.'" Ron said, "Oh yeah, he's got the real deal."

My dad said, "I understand baptism doesn't save you. The cross saves you." But it was an ordinance he wanted to follow. On October 31, 1998, he stood in front of the church. My dad, who was not going to come to a church for his own son's wedding because it was against his honor, got baptized.

The Lord called him in March of 1999, and he was 78 when he passed. All of these Turks from Chicago came to his funeral, and I eulogized my dad as did a couple of his buddies at the chapel. These guys were probably saying, "Wait a minute. *Mehmet became a Christian?* You're kidding."

It was an incredible journey for my parents and me, and make no mistake—it was a journey. After I gave my life to Christ, I still tried to have it both ways. I was kind of like a Secret Service Christian, and no one really knew except for me and God. One day Hollis Haff, the Steelers' chaplain, spoke about walking the talk. Jesus said to his disciples: "If you are ashamed of me here on Earth before this adulterous generation, I would be ashamed of you in front of the Father." I said to myself, *I'm ashamed of my faith.* Then Hollis talked about, "Are you straddling the fence?"

I was still drinking and I was going to Bible study, and one thing about straddling the fence is you get chafed pretty bad. Galatians 6:7 says, "Do not be deceived. God shall not be mocked. What a man sows, so he shall reap." I thought, *Am I mocking God? I am. I'm trying to have it both ways.* In the Book of Revelations, there is a warning to Laodicea, one of the seven churches of Revelations: "I wish you were hot or I wish you were cold, but since you are lukewarm, I will spit you out of my mouth." That was me. I was lukewarm. He spoke to my heart and said, "Tunch, it's time. You need to be with me wholeheartedly. Quit pretending."

I am very open about my faith and I will tell anyone about Jesus and pray for them. Jesus said, "I am the way, the truth, and the life. Nobody gets to the Father but through me." I know that for the first 25 years of my life my heart was hardened to that. But then when I finally realized that Jesus is who He said He is, it changed me.

The beauty of the Lord is he a god of second chances. And not only does he give us a second chance to know Him, He also calls on us to be part of his work here on Earth. He tells Peter and Peter's brother, Andrew, "Follow me and I will make you fishers of men." How cool is that? The God of the universe would call on us to be part of what He's doing here on Earth—in spite of our pasts. If God could use a knucklehead like me, then he could use anybody. And I praise him for that.

Acknowledgments

First and foremost, I want to thank my Lord Jesus Christ. I know that it is only by His grace that I played in the National Football League and I know that he put me with the Pittsburgh Steelers so I could see the Lord in the lives of so many of my teammates, and that was how I met Jesus. I want to thank my brother Craig Wolfley for his contributions to this book. We've been best friends since we met each other in 1980. Not only was he a great teammate and a great linemate, he is a great friend and a brother in the Lord. We have shared so much together over the years in football and in life, and he's been there every step of the way.